STAYING SOLVENT

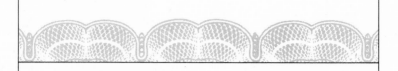

STAYING SOLVENT

A Comprehensive Guide to Equal Credit for Women

Emily Card, Ph.D.

Holt, Rinehart and Winston

New York

Library of Congress Cataloging in Publication Data
Card, Emily.
Staying solvent.
Includes index.
1. Sex discrimination in consumer credit—United
States. 2. Credit—United States. 3. Women—Finance,
Personal. I. Title.
HG3756.U54C39   1984   332.7'43   84-4537
ISBN 0-03-062954-3

First Edition

Designed by Lucy Albanese
Printed in the United States of America
1   3   5   7   9   10   8   6   4   2

Grateful acknowledgment is made to TRW, Inc., for
permission to reprint their Updated Credit Profile.

ISBN 0-03-062954-3

Dedicated

To Mama
Anne America Dempsey Watts
1916–1984

Much missed for her inspiration
and wisdom

Contents

Acknowledgments

This book spans ten years of work on my part as well as on the part of many others, so the list of people to be properly thanked is necessarily long.

First, my chance to make a contribution to equal credit would never have occurred if Senator Bill Brock from Tennessee, the bill's main sponsor, had not first selected me as a Fellow in his office, then given the bill and my work on it a tremendous amount of time and energy. Not only did Senator Brock devote long hours, he brought tremendous political subtlety to the bill's passage, which I believe would have been difficult, if not impossible, to achieve without him.

Not only did Bill Brock actively sponsor the legislation, but he was willing to give a staffer, in this case myself, a much more visible and active role than is often the case. His generosity in sharing the credit and the limelight has shaped my subsequent work with the law.

During passage, many people provided moral support.

Most of them have been mentioned in chapter 2 of the book, but here I want to add a note about the work of the late Robert Bruce Satterthwait who helped prepare the original research.

Later when I decided to do follow-up work on the legislation by founding the Women's Credit and Finance Project, I received institutional support from the Program for the Study of Women and Men in Society at the University of Southern California, from Donna Shalala at the U.S. Department of Housing and Urban Development, and from the Kennedy School of Government at Harvard University. In particular at Harvard, Governor Michael Dukakis, then at Harvard between his two administrations, provided his sponsorship, encouragement, and guidance. Also at the Kennedy School, fellow student Dorothy Sable helped answer hotline questions. Earlier, at USC many interns contributed their time to the credit project, but in particular Regina Steele was with me the first day we opened our doors and with her legal training provided firsthand assistance in handling cases.

Throughout the period of the credit project, Attorney Stephen Spataro was of counsel and donated many hours to consumers in need.

The project received financial support from many private donors, including Anna Bing Arnold, Ed Asner, Martin Harmon, Norman and Frances Lear, Charles Manatt and the First Los Angeles Bank, Stewart Mott, Joan Palevsky, Helen Reddy, Vicci Sperry, and Jeff Wald.

And much of the tremendous volume of mail was handled with the help of my mother, to whom the book is dedicated. Since she never had a separate financial identity until late in life, she was pleased to work on helping other women.

During the book writing itself, Marietta Battaglia White and Judith Lutz helped organize the research and made editorial contributions in the early stage. Roger Goldblatt, the former

Associate Director of the White House Office of Consumer Affairs, helped gather research in Washington. Susan McHenry of *Ms.* magazine worked very hard to bring the final version of the book into shape. Lucille Johnson, my high-school English teacher, who always encouraged my writing, took time to correct my grammar once again.

Warren Dennis, a Washington-based attorney who has been a friend since the Hills days and who is one of the top legal experts on the Equal Credit Opportunity Act, commented in detail about the legal portions of the book. Barbara Arnold, formerly head of the Cincinnati office of the FTC and now in private practice in Los Angeles, also reviewed the law portions. Professor Grace Blumberg of the UCLA Law School and W. S. McClanahan, author of a text on community property law, also read the manuscript, as did two other attorneys who, because of agency positions, asked to remain unnamed. All of these persons provided tremendous assistance, and their time in so commenting is greatly appreciated, although any remaining mistakes in interpretation are my own.

My agent, Denise Marcil, has been especially generous, and I want to thank my editors, Bobbi Mark and Yvonne Torstensson.

Over the years, I have received enormous support from the women's movement for my work. In particular, a list of thanks would not be complete without mention of Gloria Steinem, who has often picked up the phone or dropped me a note at just the right moment. Though such moments are rare enough to be a privilege, Gloria has always managed to have perfect timing.

My family has all lent support. My two grandmothers, Avie Williams Watts and Bertha Carmichael Dempsey, provided important models of women of accomplishment. My father, Ray Watts, lent his house for a month during the final stages of writing. Both my sisters, Judy Watts Colby and Janie Watts Spataro, contributed their own professional editorial and research expertise, and my brother, Dean Watts, has always been willing to share his business insights into the informal workings of credit. Over the years Lamar Card has always challenged me to reach higher.

The Electronic Cottage in Ojai, California, typed the first version of the manuscript, and then Nicole Runkle worked long and hard typing and researching the final version.

Finally, my list ends where an author's list often does, with my husband, Kent Brosveen, who helped so much at every stage.

STAYING SOLVENT

Introduction

At the very center of women's attempts to gain control over their lives is the attempt to gain control over their finances. With more women working and more expected to enter the work force each year, women cannot afford to be second-class citizens financially. They must learn the traditional financial wisdom as well as be prepared for the brave new world of tomorrow.

For tomorrow, as today, you will need money. And if, by chance, you don't have much money, you'd better have the next best thing—the poor woman's capital—good credit.

Simply put, credit is the ability to pay later for obligations incurred today. Our maxim, "A penny saved is a penny earned," suggests that people who use credit are not quite as wise as people who don't. But business people and the wealthy have always used credit. In fact, capital generally cannot be accumulated in this society without credit.

Your credit is the basis for almost every financial transaction in which you participate. Even when you are paying for your groceries at a supermarket by check, your credit—in the form of a check-cashing card or credit card—is the validation for your check, which is really a cash instrument. Forget attitudes that put you down for needing to use credit. Credit is not a bad thing; in fact, you need it.

The very word comes from the Latin verb *credere*, "to believe." Your credit represents the sum total of belief in your financial capacity by the financial community. A healthy credit rating is the next best thing to being born rich. A person who does not have credit at all cannot hope to compete economically with large-scale enterprises that take credit for granted and build credit costs even into items bought for cash.

The aim of my book is to take the mystery out of credit and to show you, the average woman consumer, how to use credit as part of your financial base. I have chosen the title *Staying Solvent* to distinguish this money book from those that focus on the notion of "getting rich." The point is to emphasize that while we cannot all get rich, we can all at least stay solvent.

The credit climate for women has changed dramatically since I set foot in Washington a decade ago and began work on the Equal Credit Opportunity Act as a United States Senate Fellow for Senator Bill Brock (R-Tennessee). In 1973, it was not only commonplace to deny women credit, it was thought to be good business practice.

The Equal Credit Opportunity Act was passed in October 1974. Today, financial institutions recognize the women's market as one of the fastest growing. Still, everywhere I go, women tell me of their continuing difficulties getting credit. Thus a decade of credit rights and increased visibility has not produced credit equality for women.

Just as I was completing *Staying Solvent*, I took a vacation to gather momentum for the final editing. I had just spent a long summer in New York taping my television series on consumer finance, so I needed a break from the topic of women and money. The first evening, hoping to avoid too much business discussion, I sat down to dinner at a large round communal table at the hotel. After we had exchanged names and occupations, the woman to my right turned to me and said: "Do I have a story for you!" She then proceeded to tell me of her long struggle to get credit, concluding with a tale of her dealings with American Express. She had twice been denied an American Express card as "Marvine Brown," but one day she came home and found in her Beverly Hills mailbox a solicitation from American Express addressed to "M. Brown." She sent the solicitation in, and sure enough the card came back to "Mr. M. Brown."

None of the salient financial facts about her had changed, just her sex.

Recently, American Express lost a major suit for violating the part of the Equal Credit Opportunity Act that says you cannot discriminate on the basis of marital status. American Express revoked the card of a woman when she became a widow. She decided to sue and won her case. The law says creditors cannot automatically cancel an account when a customer changes her marital status without demonstrating a change in her willingness or ability to pay.

Ironically, American Express is also making one of the biggest efforts to reach out to women, who, along with young professionals, have been targeted as a major new market.

How could a responsible and forward-thinking company like American Express, which spends advertising dollars so generously to woo women, end up getting sued for violating the antidiscrimination-in-credit law? It doesn't make good business sense, yet this sort of thing occurs every day—and in other companies besides American Express.

The Bank of America in California provides another case in

3

point. In 1983, the bank, the largest in the United States, used Visa and MasterCard application forms that specifically violated the Equal Credit Opportunity Act. Here's how.

The law provides that you must be able to use your husband's or former husband's credit history for any account for which you are or have been held liable. (Under California community property laws, a woman is by definition liable on any personal, nonbusiness account her husband holds.) Yet, Bank of America's application had a box for the spouse's signature authorizing the bank to obtain her/his credit report if relying on community property, even though the law provides the right to rely on that credit history without having to get a spouse's permission.

This questionable application was drawn to my attention by a woman who had heard me speak and was so fired up about getting her own credit identity that she went right out, got an application, and brought the completed form back for my review.

Ironically, the Bank of America is the institution that had originally drawn my own attention to women's credit. In 1968, as a young lecturer at the University of California, I tried to obtain one of the (then new) BankAmericards. I submitted an application, reflecting my substantial earnings and including the information that my husband was a full-time student and therefore not currently employed.

Back came the application, with this letter:

> Since you are married, we cannot give you an application in your own name. If your husband [the unemployed student, mind you] would like a card, we are enclosing an application for him.

I saved this letter.

My first day on the job as a Senate Fellow in 1973, the National Commission on Consumer Finance issued a report on consumer credit. The first official acknowledgment that credit discrimination was a problem for women appeared in two pages of the three-hundred-page report.

I approached Senator Brock to discuss the issue. We talked about the fact that women were entering the work force in record numbers. Many were creditworthy, yet few were obtaining credit. The thinking of financial institutions had not caught up with the times, and it was obvious just from the response to the report that a special effort was needed. It appeared that legislation would be necessary to give women credit access commensurate with our economic roles.

I began writing the proposal for Senator Brock that January. In July the result of that proposal, the Equal Credit Opportunity Act, won its first legislative battle. It was signed into law in October 1974, making it unlawful for a creditor to discriminate on the basis of sex or marital status. In 1976, Congress strengthened the law further by adding prohibitions against discrimination on the basis of race, color, religion, national origin, and age, provided that one is old enough to contract. Then how could a large institution like the Bank of America, with hundreds of thousands of customers, get away with disregard for the law in 1983?

Sometimes, there is a gap between an institution's policy and its procedure. A policy may be correct, but people lower down on the chain may not understand it or abide by it. I'll never forget the day my own bank president called to tell me a clerk asked for her husband's cosignature on a credit application. She simply called the manager and set the matter right. But she was a particularly informed consumer who was confident of her rights.

In other cases, institutions—rightly or wrongly—believe that certain additional protection is needed to collect their debt. Interpretations of the law by their legal staffs allow them to feel safe stretching both the letter and spirit of the law until a persistent consumer challenges them in court. Remember the court challenge that changed American Express's policy.

What about those Bank of America forms? How did they get off Bank of America's counters in 1983? Upon discovering the form, I called the bank's excellent public affairs officer, and told him how surprised I was to see such a form. In a few hours, he called back with a response from the legal department at the bank's headquarters. In fact, the illegal form was a "mistake" and "outdated." Supposedly, the form, printed in 1982, had been replaced. Yet my consumer had found it. Except for our chance meeting, she, like many other consumers, would have been intimidated by the form and would possibly have forgone the opportunity to apply. The Bank of America avoided a legal confrontation, but I wouldn't be surprised to see another large institution caught in the same boat.

But legal battles are expensive and time-consuming. The Equal Credit Opportunity Act's damages and attorney fee provisions aren't big enough to encourage many attorneys to take an Equal Credit Opportunity Act rights case on a contingency. And not many women have the resources to go to court when they are wrongfully denied credit.

Complaining to the government does not work very well either. Federally mandated regulations that appear on credit applications were meant to offer specific places for consumers to complain if they felt they were having a problem. But writing to the government doesn't promise quick action. Today, the trend is toward less, not more, government help for consumers.

Knowing your own rights will protect you in most credit situations. If you confidently assert your rights, a law-breaking creditor will often relent. An employee caught off base will quickly listen to reason when you are ready to go to the head of the organization to present your facts.

If you know your rights, you can take preventive action, such as making sure you have credit in your own name, checking your credit report, and managing your credit effectively.

Whether you're a homemaker or a celebrity, you can't take credit for granted. It's part of women's socialization not to feel comfortable about money. Even a woman like Gloria Steinem, who has played such a leading role in changing all our lives, has not attended to her own personal financial matters. Gloria recently shared some of her experiences about credit in her office at *Ms.* magazine.

My first question was whether she had seen her own credit report. She hadn't. Then I asked her whether she thought she had a credit file, given her limited use of credit. She responded, "I don't know. This is an interesting question, because I have never bought a car or a house, I've never borrowed money, never had a mortgage. Whether or not it exists just with credit cards, I don't know. What do you think, does it?"

Gloria may not in fact have a credit file. I wondered whether her family had used credit. "My family was always in debt. My father was a great wheeler-dealer and a dreamer and not overwhelmingly practical. I spent a lot of my childhood sitting in the waiting room of Household Finance while he chatted with some loan officer. The fact that father was always in debt was a great source of anxiety to my mother as she was very, very worried about money."

I asked her whether, as she'd gotten older, she'd seen any shifts in her credit attitudes. Gloria replied, "I think that now since I have more confidence in my ability to earn, I am willing to borrow money and actually get into debt. But up to now that's something I've never done."

We learn many of our money attitudes from our parents, and most of us had parents who, one way or another, reflected the traditional notion that the man was in charge of the money.

Though he had bad credit habits, Gloria's father played the

traditional money decision-maker role, if only by incurring debts. Her mother played the traditional passive woman's role of worrying rather than becoming actively involved.

If it took a woman as brave as Gloria Steinem forty-nine years to overcome her childhood programming and feel comfortable with credit, no wonder the rest of us need help!

That's why I wrote this book—to give every woman the tools she needs to take charge of her credit life. While books on finances abound, this is the first ever that gives basic advice to women on how to create a credit identity, and then how to maintain that credit skillfully and with a minimum of fuss.

For the past decade, I've been privileged to serve as a participant-observer on the national credit rights scene, first on Capitol Hill, then later as chair of a task force for President Carter's campaign. With government contracts, university support, and private contributions, I organized the Consumer Credit and Finance Project and the Women's Credit Rights Project Hotline, housed first at the University of Southern California and then at Harvard University.

Through my research, I found that the problems identified in the early 1970s had been replaced by new sets of concerns. Marital status discrimination had become more subtle, and new tactics were needed if women were to benefit fully from the law. At Harvard, I completed the research report that provides the basis for this book. (All names in the case histories have been changed.)

The book is designed for you—whether you have lots of credit now and just want to be more informed, or whether you have absolutely no credit and are not sure you even want it.

A book cannot take the place of a finance course or offer the thorough socialization that has allowed many men to understand the world of finance for generations, but it can place you in a position to have an understanding of the finance system and your rights within it.

Even those who have successfully gone through the credit application process in the past and dealt with credit matters find it hard to remember the details months or years later when the situation arises again. "What was it I should do if I am asked my marital status when applying for credit?" "How do I handle being turned down for credit when no reason is given?" "If I have to choose between paying the Sears bill or American Express, which credit is it better to keep intact?"

We often develop fear and loathing of subjects like credit, which seem awash in bureaucratic detail, and hence difficult to pin down. It's a frame of mind that encourages putting off taking care of things that should be attended to. This book might not inspire you to love the details that require your attention when establishing and maintaining good credit, but I hope it will answer your questions. My purpose is to give you the equipment and credit information you need. Getting it right the first time saves you lots of wear and tear.

Credit manuals often tend to be formal and legalistic. If they address the situation of women at all, they often present your rights as if the law will enforce itself.

Women and men alike need a more informal, how-to-do-it approach. To provide that, the book is organized around four functional themes:

> Understanding Credit (Part One)
> Your Legal Rights (Part Two)
> Getting Credit (Part Three), and
> Maximizing Credit (Part Four)

While the book is based on women's experiences and women's special needs, particularly those that arise from the divergent effects of marriage on women and men, much of the information on how the credit system works presented here has not appeared elsewhere, so I encourage men to read on, too.

I thought long and hard about whether I should make this book gender free, but since my main concerns are those of women, who have the most critical need for this information, I decided to write the book as you find it—aimed at women but valid for men. If you are a male reader, you'll have unwittingly provided yourself with an additional learning bonus: firsthand experience of a world in which everything is written with "she," not "he." Women have had to make the opposite adjustment for years.

There is no such thing as taking your credit for granted. The subliminal message of the last few decades may have been that with modern credit cards there is nothing to it. But anyone who has ever felt trapped by too little or too much credit knows that this isn't so.

Even if you do have a fairly substantial income, you cannot charge everything and hope that eventually you will be able to pay. Debts usually require constant monthly attention. But debt can build up over time, especially if you are going through a difficult period. Some debts are virtually free to the consumer, whereas others have stiff penalties for paying too late or too soon.

But, the stiffest penalties of all are paid by women who have no ability to incur a debt at all—that is, those who have no access to credit.

If we women are going to achieve the expertise about the world of finance that many men have enjoyed for years, we have to play catch-up. Since time and energy as well as money are at a premium, whatever "know-how" is required to preserve them has found its way into this book.

Most importantly, we all must learn to appreciate why it is worthwhile taking such care with our credit. America is now entering an era more closely resembling the forties and early fifties than the careless affluence of the last thirty years. Economic growth is slowing, recession and inflation have had their impact, and consumers are paying much higher prices for credit. In 1978, real estate books suggested, quite correctly for the time, that any real estate investment was bound to grow since interest rates were lower than the rate of inflation. These books are now dated and obsolete. And, credit is not as easy to obtain as it was a few years ago. "Easy credit" is a thing of the past.

Some analysts have suggested we are seeing the Europeanization of America: a period of declining disposable income that will make it particularly valuable to learn skills of financial management that will keep our hard-earned money working for us longer. As the cost of money fluctuates—that is, as the interest rates rise and fall—knowing the difference between a good and a bad credit decision and what exactly makes some credit purchases pay off becomes more important than ever.

Good credit—and anything you pay a stiff price for ought to be good—does benefit from proper care. If you've ever looked enviously at someone who slips out her gold American Express card at lunch and pays the bill, even though you happen to know that the card-carrier is "between jobs," you know what I mean.

However critical credit is today, it will become even more imperative to participate in the financial life of the 1990s. If all of our outstanding obligations came due today, how many of us could actually pay them? Very few people, yet this is the exact situation that we can look forward to as the financial world moves toward the "debit card" and electronic transactions.

The debit card will be the card that takes money directly out of your account at the point of purchase. Obviously, adjustments will have to be made for this new aspect of the financial future. Most of us will probably engage in many of our financial transactions right from our computer terminals at home. These and many other new developments will depend on one's credit and financial standing.

What will this mean for the average middle-class woman? Hopefully, the same thing it will mean for men. I look forward to the day when more women will be able to say, as a friend of mine recently did, in complaining about her ailing resort business: "I was down to my last ten thousand dollars." What average middle-class woman wouldn't welcome such a problem?

But first, let's get equal!

FIVE-POINT QUIZ

Now what about you? Is it worthwhile for you to brave the credit system? Here's a five-point quiz to help you determine whether you have enough credit.

1. If you found yourself suddenly without income, could you survive for three months using existing lines of credit and credit cards?

2. If your refrigerator broke, could you easily charge a new one?

3. Can you cash a check virtually anywhere?

4. Can you always be assured that the credit cards in your wallet work for any normal situation of day-to-day living, or do you have to go from store to store to find the credit card that will work for the situation?

5. If you were given a job assignment and asked to travel to a distant city immediately, even though it was Sunday night, and there was no time for the company to issue you an advance check, could you cover all necessary expenses with the plastic in your pocket?

Part One

UNDER-
STANDING
CREDIT

1

The Growth of Credit

One bright sunny California morning, I was sitting at my desk in my study preparing for a hectic day of meetings connected by long drives on the Los Angeles freeways. It was the kind of morning on which you feel a bit behind before you even start the day. So I was bothered when at 8:00 A.M. the phone rang. The caller was a woman with a credit problem.

I tried to shorten my discussion with her so that I could hurry on my way to my "more important" meetings. Then, feeling guilty for being ungracious, I stopped myself and realized that nothing was more important than taking the time to discuss this woman's concern.

The woman's voice was frantic.

"I've been married twenty-four and a half years. I have no credit. On Tuesday, my husband returned from a business trip. He handed me a letter with a check for five hundred dollars in it. The letter said he wanted a divorce and the

15

money would have to tide me over until something could be arranged. He closed all of our store credit accounts and our checking account. He put his weekly paycheck in a separate account, had our safety deposit box number changed, and then closed our Visa account and took away the gas card.

"Next week he is leaving on a business trip to Hawaii for two weeks and I can't get a lawyer to work fast enough to straighten things out. Besides, I have only five hundred dollars to last indefinitely, and our lawyer and all the other lawyers require a retainer even though they said that what my husband did was illegal. I'm afraid to spend any money on anything because I don't even have a gas card. I am not sure if I spend my gas driving to an attorney that I'll have food money in three weeks."

"What about the Women's Legal Clinic?" I asked.

"I contacted them yesterday, but I'll still have to pay something if they take my case. Even though my husband's income is six hundred and sixty dollars a week, I can't afford a lawyer!"

"Do you have any children who could help?"

"Yes, my eldest son would try to get me a gas credit card, but I'm worried because he tends to run up his bills and they may not let him cosign."

Even though Mrs. Williams had been married twenty-five years, her husband earned $35,000 a year (half of which was legally hers under California law) and she had enjoyed a decent life-style, she had no financial identity of her own. All the rights in the world were no good to her. She needed help fast. If she had had credit cards in her own name, she would at least have been able to cope better with her extremely difficult situation.

It was too late for me to help Mrs. Williams. All I could do was offer her psychological support and refer her to a sympathetic attorney. Once her current crisis was over, I hoped she would take time to get credit.

It is not too late, though, for you. No reader of this book should ever have to face what Mrs. Williams did.

Our modern economy is inconceivable without consumer credit. Yet, women frequently find themselves exactly in that position, excluded from the modern credit arena. Americans expect to buy and pay later. Until very recently, most women's participation was indirect through their spouses, like Mrs. Williams's. Her continued participation in the system was at her husband's pleasure and she could be cut off at any moment by him. The system frequently presumes that the man is in charge of credit even in a two-earner family.

One woman caller had filed for credit using her salary, which was the primary source of household income. Even though she earned more than her husband, the cards were sent in his name. She used the account for a while and paid the bill regularly. Then he discovered the bill in the mailbox one day and canceled the account. She had not missed a payment, so she called the creditor expecting that the firm would reinstate the account once it was understood that the account had mistakenly been issued in his name. Instead, they demanded that she reapply.

Where did this pervasive system from which women were frequently excluded come from?

Let's look at the growth of credit. However, if you have a current credit crisis of your own, skip right to chapter 3.

As you can see from Table 1 on page 18, consumer credit has grown steadily. But, until the passage of the Equal Credit

Opportunity Act in 1974, "consumers" equaled "men." In the ten years since women were given credit rights, outstanding credit has more than tripled. Based on the figures, it's evident that the "women's market" represented a large pool of pent-up demand.

Table 1. GROWTH OF CONSUMER CREDIT IN THE U.S.
IN MILLIONS OF DOLLARS

	1943	1949	1959	1969	1979	1983 (Sept.)
Total Credit	6,101	20,295	59,432	135,431	377,486	455,449

Source: Federal Reserve System, Division of Research and Statistics.

Although credit has grown rapidly in recent years, it is not, as many people assume, either a recent phenomenon or a phenomenon of advanced industrial society. Sometimes we are tempted to think of credit as if it appeared at the same time as the automobile, but it's been around much longer.

All through history, farmers have had to rely on credit in one form or another to tide them over between seasons and weather cycles. Thus, credit has been used in many forms and in many societies to smooth out income fluctuations.

Two early modern forms of credit were used to create economic "ties that bind," ensuring that the colonial farmer and factory worker were tied by debt to the economy. With the growth of export crop economies all over the colonial world, including the American colonies, local farmers bought their goods at exporter-owned stores that would extend them credit for manufactured goods against purchasing their entire crop at the end of the year. The same sort of system also developed in factory towns, where the factory workers would buy their goods at the "company store." The amount owed would be deducted from their wages, an early example of a "debit" system. These practices kept people in place, working to pay for what they had already spent. Sound familiar?

Modern consumer credit began to develop in the period after the 1800s. Dramatic economic changes took place in the mid-1860s after the Civil War. As large numbers of people were drawn from farms to cities, manufacturing industries grew rapidly and many department stores and chain retail institutions were founded.

After World War I, there was another surge in credit buying, caused by a postwar boom and a need to finance the newly popular automobile. Automobile manufacturers could not sell their cars because lack of cash prevented customers from purchasing their products, so they developed corporations to finance the retail contracts.

By the late 1920s some larger banks had entered the consumer loan business on an experimental basis, but bankers lived up to their conservative image. Although these experiments were observed by bankers across the country, few were willing to accept consumer lending activity as a viable bank service because it was based on a new concept of creditworthiness. Bankers usually looked at net worth on a financial statement—the "bottom line"—and tangible collateral, but middle-income consumers couldn't match these standards. Instead, consumers offered an expected steady income stream backed up by "vocational ability" and character.

In 1934, money for home repair entered the scene. The Federal Housing Administration (FHA) announced that it would furnish a liberal guarantee for home repair and modernization loans. The FHA program was a major factor influencing banks to enter the consumer credit field because conservative bankers now had government protection against default.

This experience, in turn, furnished convincing proof to bankers that installment credit would be extended to qualified individuals on a safe and profitable basis. By 1938, almost four thousand banks were engaged in some form of consumer credit.

In the period after World War II, consumer credit again grew rapidly. In 1943, credit outstanding was $6.1 billion. By 1949, it had grown to $20.3 billion and by 1959, it stood at $59.4 billion. The same pattern was repeated after the Vietnam War period, from $135.4 billion in 1969 to $377.5 billion in 1979. By 1983, outstanding consumer credit had grown to $455.5 billion.

Changing consumer incomes and life-styles, postwar expansion of government loan guarantees, a changing economy, and the entrance of women into the system all contributed to the rise in total consumer credit since World War II and the addition of new forms of credit.

Consumers' ability to repay debts depends in part upon the expected size of their incomes. In the twenty-one years between 1950 and 1971, incomes jumped tremendously and the same trends have continued. Income has not only increased but it also has become more stable because of the development of unemployment benefits, health insurance, and the participation of women in two-earner families. The greater participation of women in the labor force provided both an impetus for more credit and a rationale for our right to have it. In 1950, only 24 percent of married women worked, by 1976 the number had risen to 51 percent, and the government projects that by 1990, 75 percent of married women will hold jobs. Certainly these working women, as much as any other single factor, added to the demand for credit.

Another factor that encouraged consumers' use of credit

was the increased urbanization of the population. Over 15 percent of the total population was living on farms in 1950, but less than 5 percent was by 1970, and by 1980, the number had declined to 2.6 percent.

On the farm, people are much less dependent on cash. They can often make do with what they have on hand. I remember my own grandmother's cellar full of potatoes that fed us through the winter, potatoes that she herself had grown in her kitchen garden during the summer. But in a city you cannot go down to your cellar and get the potatoes that you grew last summer. You must pay cash for what you eat. Money often arrives on a schedule different from your needs, thus creating a greater dependence on cash income.

Urban life-style is also different, with many more accessible things to buy. As desire to buy increases, so does the desire for credit. In the fifties, as the final wave of people moved to the cities for the first time, people were newly exposed to urban "goodies." Today television makes all of us, farm and city folks alike, "urban consumers."

The increased use of credit is also explained by the changing age distribution of the population. The traditional wisdom is that the more young people there are in a population, the more credit is likely to be used because credit permits them to pay for purchases to meet current needs out of expected future higher income. Between 1950 and 1971, the number of individuals eighteen to twenty-four years old grew about 50 percent, whereas the number of individuals in all other age brackets grew by only 35 percent. This "baby boom" contributed tremendously to the growth in credit to meet the demands for goods and services by a burgeoning crop of young Americans. As this baby boom population ages and the age balance shifts upward into the 1990s, there may be some correlated slowing of credit demands if historical patterns hold.

Over time, consumers have increasingly bought more durable consumer goods like refrigerators and other consumer-owned "capital goods" such as automobiles.

Let's look at the major asset consumers have acquired —homes. Partly as a result of federal FHA and Veterans Administration (VA) programs supporting mortgages, and because of growth in incomes and the attractiveness of real estate, consumers have bought more houses. The percentage of owner-occupied homes rose from 55 percent in 1950 to 64 percent in 1970, where it leveled off by the 1980 census. Women and singles have entered the market in the last few years, and now account for 16 percent of owner-occupied homes.

Along with home ownership came suburbanization. Homeowners, especially in the suburbs, tend to buy refrigerators, washing machines, lawn mowers, power tools, and often a second car. Between 1960 and 1971, the proportion of households owning two or more cars jumped from about 16 percent to just under 30 percent. By 1980, the figure was 34 percent two-car households and 18 percent three-car households.

The shift to asset ownership is also reflected by consumer decision to substitute personally owned "capital goods" for commercially owned ones. For example, people purchased automobiles rather than pay for fares on streetcars and buses owned by the government or transportation companies. This shift meant consumers needed credit, since cars usually are too expensive to buy outright.

Likewise, people purchased washing machines and dryers rather than spending money in Laundromats. They substituted owning a television set for admission to movies and other forms of entertainment. Credit was needed for all of these purchases.

And if, over time, they saved money by owning their own washer and dryer, then these savings would free up more money to buy yet other "capital goods." In turn, this purchasing created additional demands for consumer credit.

The trend to asset ownership was also aided by the movement of women into the labor force. As women became busier outside the home, we were able to get more timesavers in the home, such as automatic dishwashers and other home appliances. Now, as Americans consume more than one-third of their meals outside the home, there's a shift again, so home appliances may become less important, but home computers may take their place as the new imperative timesaver.

The growth of credit in our economy has often been associated with a new surge of consumer buying after a major war. This has held true after the Civil War, World War I, World War II, and the Vietnam War. The phenomenal growth of credit in the 1970s was connected to the Vietnam War as well as to the entry of women into the market.

The continued growth of credit along with inflation in the ten years from 1969 to 1979 led to action by the Board of Governors of the Federal Reserve System (the Fed) in the fall of 1979, when the board initiated a series of steps to curb consumer credit spending in order to combat inflation. With some initial actions taken in October 1979, and the imposition in March 1980 of consumer credit controls, the American public received the signal that credit was no longer a "good thing." When the Fed lifted the controls in July 1980, the American consumer had learned an important lesson in the intervening six months: The availability of consumer credit could no longer be taken for granted.

Women were especially appalled. Since we had only recently gained the right to expect credit in 1974, we wanted our chance to use it rather than be told, just as we'd entered the system, that it was being cut back.

Despite the urging of the government that consumers curb their spending, consumers had also learned another lesson. Without credit in an inflationary period, consumers would suffer even more. For example, many consumers kept pace with this record inflation only through home ownership. Women and minorities, who had not been able to get credit, found themselves even further behind in the inflation scenario.

In ten years, the decade spanning the early 1970s until the early eighties, the government had come full circle in its attitude toward consumer protection legislation. The federal budget director denounced consumer protection advocates in *The Wall Street Journal*. People who continued to favor credit for consumers were seen as being against economic recovery. For a few months, consumer advocates found ourselves defending consumers' right to have credit.

Efforts to erode consumers' interest in credit usually go against the American historical grain. Credit has become an ordinary component of financial transactions in our society. We take it for granted. If consumers are asked to give up credit, then business must be asked to sacrifice it as well, or consumers will be disproportionately affected in terms of both inflation and tax savings.

Credit is built into our tax system. There are significant tax advantages to using credit, which have also served to help the growth of credit. And, since money paid back in tomorrow's dollars is always cheaper than spending today's, the use of credit is central to sound financial planning—and making money.

The growth of the credit system occurred without the full participation of women. Until 1974, most women participated only indirectly, through their spouses, if at all. Most of the popular kinds of credit were created before women entered the system, so they were aimed at an essentially "male only" market. Revolving charge accounts were established as early as 1938, the first travel card in 1950, the first bank charge card in 1951, and overdraft protection in the mid-1950s. All these being so, a couple of points follow.

Does a credit system invented by men, for men, really work to best advantage for women? No. Are there aspects to the system that need to change to fit women better? Yes!

There are some key parallels between the credit system and the employment system. Both penalize women for dropping out of the work force to raise families. Just as loss of seniority and loss of continuous experience result in discontinuities in employment, so too in credit. Credit is expected to grow steadily as you take each step up the age and earnings ladders. An interruption can cause a woman to lose her credit completely. Afterward it's hard, in your forties, to convince creditors to view you as an appropriately responsible adult. After all, how could you arrive at middle age without credit in your own name?

Second, given the growth of the system, there's a relationship between a card's "gender identity" and its value as a credit tool. Just as "male jobs" carry more clout, so does "male credit."

Credit which has been traditionally aimed at men, such as automobile credit, mortgage credit, and travel cards, carries more weight than "women's credit"—department and furniture stores, doctors, dentists, and utilities. Grocery stores, which until recently catered mostly to homemakers, usually offer no credit at all. Also, credit that has been identified with women's roles has little credit reporting and less credit clout.

How did women finally get into this burgeoning system? As credit grew, so did consumer complaints. Eventually Congress had to sit up and take notice, which it did. As a result, a series of consumer protection laws was passed in the late sixties and early seventies.

In the original Consumer Credit Protection Act, Congress mandated the presidentially appointed National Consumer Credit Commission to review consumer credit policies. As this prestigious commission sat, a handful of feminists urged it to look at women's lack of credit participation. Finally, the commission held hearings in May 1972 on the issue of sex discrimination in credit. The testimony resulted in the first official acknowledgment of women's plight.

In its December report the same year, the panel recommended that

> states undertake immediate and thorough review of the degree to which their laws inhibit the granting of credit to creditworthy women, and amend them where necessary to assure that credit is not restricted because of a person's sex.

With the commission calling only for *voluntary* effort on the states' parts to overcome creditor resistance, you can see that passing the credit law in Congress would be an uphill battle! Nevertheless the stage was set.

2

The Credit Poor: Exclusion of Women from Credit

Think back to 1968, the year the first consumer credit protection law was passed. American Express cards had been in existence for ten years, but BankAmericards were new. Women's credit rights, while a problem for individual women, were not an issue. In fact, we women were just beginning to think about our rights, and often if a woman were denied credit, she assumed something was wrong with her, not with the system. Women's pay then was 58 percent of men's (it's 60 percent now). In the professions, only 3 percent of lawyers and 10 percent of college teachers were women.

No wonder women could not effectively obtain credit on their own. No law guaranteed women access to credit. Sometimes the law even supported the system of discrimination through regulations that required creditors to treat women differently from men.

Whether a woman was single, married, widowed, divorced, or separated, there were specific constraints upon her attempts to arrange credit for herself. Single women, it was presumed, would soon be married, and once married would become pregnant and drop out of the work force. Married women were assumed to be one step closer to this fate. Widows were thought to be defenseless and in need of the protection of trustees. Divorced women were seen as unstable. So if you're having problems today, don't despair. At least the law is on our side now. Even so, some of the old horror stories still ring too true.

Whether a woman wanted to buy a house, a car, or simply to get a newfangled credit card, she hit a wall. She found she could not obtain credit without the signature of a man. Married women almost always needed their husband's signature; single women frequently needed their father's. No matter how old a single woman was, she had to find a man to vouch for her. Divorced women had to resign from the credit system. Only by catching a new, more "creditworthy" man could they hope to reenter.

Many widows choose to hide their husbands' deaths for credit purposes and to keep everything from the telephone to the oil card in their dead husbands' names. Many a deceased John Smith and Richard Doe ate meals, took round-the-world trips, made house payments, and traveled in cars. Often it seemed that "A dead man's credit is better than a live woman's."

When I arrived in Senator Bill Brock's office in January 1973, one of the first pieces of mail I found in my Senate mailbox was from the senator himself. He had served on the National Commission on Consumer Finance, and had issued a press release discussing the commission's findings on credit discrimination.

The National Commission on Consumer Finance study documented five major categories of sex discrimination:

1. Single women had more trouble obtaining credit than single men.

2. Newly married women were forced to reapply in their husband's name.
3. Creditors were unwilling to give credit to a married woman in her own name.
4. Creditors would not count the wife's income when a couple applied for credit.
5. Divorced or widowed women had trouble establishing credit.

As a newcomer to town, I had my own banking to do. A few days later, while I was waiting to open an account near my apartment on Capitol Hill, I noticed on the bank wall the equal housing opportunity logo, a house with the mathematical symbol for equal inside. Below it the headline proclaimed "Discrimination is prohibited." Then I saw the fine print: "on the basis of race, religion, creed, color, and national origin." No mention of sex.

I jotted down the complaint number and later, back at my desk, I checked it out. I proudly announced myself as "Dr. Emily Card from Senator Brock's office." Rather than give me a vague bureaucratic reply, the operator at the Federal Deposit Insurance Corporation (FDIC) switched me immediately to the policymaker who knew the answer to my question.

To the man at the other end of the wire I represented a possible opening to a heretofore closed door, for Senator Brock was a powerful member of the Senate Banking Committee and also someone who had strong clout with the banking interests.

Quickly, I was given the answer, "Sex isn't on the sign because it's not in the law." This helpful fellow then went on to explain the current discussion in Washington about the sex discrimination issue in credit. Although almost everyone agreed there was a problem, there was no agreement about the solution. Even though the law had not been amended to include sex discrimination, his agency was reviewing whether there was a way to extend the 1968 Civil Rights Act, the Fair Housing Act (also known as Title VIII) to which the sign referred, to include sex. However, this law only dealt with housing credit discrimination. Moreover, the National Committee on Consumer Finance had documented discrimination, but only called for changes in state laws, not federal legislation.

According to my expert, in May 1972 Congresswoman Bella Abzug (D-New York) had introduced three pieces of legislation aimed at rectifying the problem. In the atmosphere of the new 93rd Congress, however, it was thought "unlikely" that Congresswoman Abzug could marshal enough votes to achieve passage of the legislation.

Although this viewpoint went against my feminist grain, I listened to the civil servant's explanation without comment. To pass a major piece of legislation in Congress, he said, the member introducing it should be on the committee that had to hear it and make a recommendation to the full Congress. Between the lines, the message was clear: "You, on the other hand, are in the right kind of office."

Passage of the Equal Credit Opportunity Act (ECOA) involved preparing the research and finally gathering support for the law. It was necessary to work with members of Congress and their staffs as well as other interested parties, including women's and industry groups. The work also involved management of the legislative process itself, through the Senate Committee and Floor, and coordination between the executive branch, the White House, and the Justice Department.

As the investigation progressed, Senator Brock's initial interest turned to strong support and leadership. From his position on the Senate Banking Committee, he steadily moved the bill forward, first in Committee and then toward the Floor.

When I started my research, I used the National Commission's categories as a basis around which to organize the further evidence which Senator Brock needed to convince the United States Senate to take action. The commission's information was a scant two pages, so I had to spend hours combing through files of letters to put together a fuller picture of the problem. This is what I found:

1. SINGLE WOMEN DID NOT ENJOY FINANCIAL FREEDOM

Although single women could usually open credit accounts at retail stores, they were often held to higher standards than men when applying for bank cards or travel cards. These higher standards included length of current employment, length of time at current address, and minimum income. Single men, even male students, often had less trouble than single women in obtaining personal loans, as well.

Single women also had trouble obtaining mortgage credit because of lender prejudices. Lenders worried that single women could not perform the necessary repairs to maintain property. How many otherwise creditworthy single men, when applying for a home loan, were questioned about their carpentry, plumbing, or electrical ability? None! The assumption that men could perform these tasks while women could not is discrimination. The ability to pay for necessary maintenance would have been more to the point, yet women were frequently denied even the most cursory examination of their means.

A single woman wrote of her experience trying to obtain credit:

> Saturday morning, August 28, I spoke to a loan officer about obtaining a home mortgage loan. He gave me the current interest rate along with closing costs, etc., and

then inquired about my husband. I told him I had no husband. He then informed me that home loans were not granted to single persons without a cosigner.

I find it very difficult to believe that I was denied a loan with absolutely no information about my ability to pay. He didn't ask about my age, my work record, my salary—nothing at all pertinent to the credit information needed to obtain a loan. I was turned down solely because I am a single woman.

Mortgages would be granted to an otherwise creditworthy single woman who had a male cosignatory, no matter what his financial status. *The Wall Street Journal* reported the case of a woman in her forties who wanted to buy a house for herself and her children but could not get a mortgage without the signature of her seventy-year-old father who was living on a pension. Single men in like situations were not required to obtain cosigners, although prejudices with respect to men in the housing market were no less stereotyped. One of the early cases brought by the Housing Section of the Civil Rights Division of the Department of Justice was against a Washington, D.C., landlord who required men, but not women, to pay an additional amount for housekeeping services, on the assumption that men were "sloppy," whereas women were consistently "neat."

2. NEWLY MARRIED WOMEN
LOST CREDIT

Creditors generally required a woman, upon her marriage, to reapply for credit, and often she received it only in her husband's name. Reapplication was not asked of men when they married. When the newly married woman notified a creditor of a change in her last name, she was asked to supply pertinent information about her husband. The new applications then traditionally resulted in issuance of credit cards to her husband.

Following is a letter received in 1973 by a woman who wrote to Senator Brock.

We are in receipt of notice of your recent marriage and wish to congratulate you and your husband. We regret that we must therefore delete your BankAmericard account, which is in your maiden name. However, you will continue to be billed for any previous balance on this account, until such time as this balance has been paid in full. If you have not already done so, please return these cards as they are of no further use to you.

If you and your husband would be interested in opening a BankAmericard account in the name of your husband, we would be happy to service you.

Can you imagine the reaction if this situation happened when a man married?

Usually creditors issued cards for the new wife on the husband's previously existing accounts without any information whatsoever concerning the wife's credit standing. By contrast, women with good credit were penalized for the new husband's credit (or lack of it). In San Bernardino, California, a newly married woman had enjoyed credit for four years. She continued her same job when she married. Nothing but her marital status changed, but creditors now would not give her credit. Why? Because her husband's credit background was not sufficient. A woman would have to check her fiancé's credit before marriage if she hoped to continue as part of the credit community!

3. NO CREDIT FOR MARRIED WOMEN
IN THEIR OWN NAMES

Creditors were often unwilling to extend credit to a married woman in her own name. Credit cards were customarily issued in the husband's name with signature privileges extended to an anonymous wife. An attorney wrote to a Chattanooga lender:

> My client Mary Stanton applied in her own name for a BankAmericard. Instead of issuing a card to Mrs. Stanton, you issued a card to her husband.
>
> Mrs. Stanton has an excellent credit reputation; she is employed. I know of no reason why her credit will not warrant the issuance of such a card, particularly since you send a BankAmericard out with very little credit check to almost every man in Chattanooga.

And despite notions to the contrary, issuance of a credit card in her married name (Mrs. John Stanton) did not mean that a woman had obtained credit in her own name. Here are a few examples:

> In Memphis, a married woman was unable to obtain credit in her own name. She was refused a bank card until her husband's application was approved.
>
> Neither she nor her husband, both twenty-one, had previously established credit. While she had been employed for nine months with First National Bank of Memphis, her husband had been employed with United Paint Company for five months. His application was approved.

A similar incident was experienced by a woman in New York.

For the past ten years of her twenty-one working years, she had earned well over $10,000 a year. [The median annual salary in 1970 was just over $7,000.] Although she maintained charge accounts in good standing in major department stores and had a savings account with over $1,000, another major department store required her husband's business address and employer's name before she would be granted credit.

A married woman in Bloomington, Indiana, had a similar story.

The woman was the family's principal wage earner and her husband was a graduate student. She maintained credit cards in her own name with several major oil companies, department stores, BankAmericard, and United Airlines. When she applied to L. S. Ayres and Company in Indianapolis, a card was issued jointly to "Mr. and Mrs." Since she had not requested her husband's inclusion, she inquired why the card bore his name. L. S. Ayres answered that "only joint cards in the husband's name are issued to married women."

4. WIFE'S INCOME NOT COUNTED

With young married couples, no matter what their background, the wife's income was not fully recognized.

Lenders operated with a "rule of thumb" that discounted the wife's income according to certain fairly standardized formulae. In marriages of less than five years, or if the wife had been working only a short time, no recognition was given to her income. If a wife between the ages of twenty-six and thirty-five were classified as a "professional," a lender counted half of her income. Only if she were over thirty-five could she receive full credit. If the wife were in a nonprofessional occupation, usually no allowance was made for her income up to age thirty-five, half allowance was given between ages thirty-five and forty-two, and full credit beyond that age.

For example, in February 1973, a Veterans Administration (VA) bulletin outlined factors to consider in deciding whether to count a wife's income for a veteran to qualify for a VA-guaranteed mortgage. These included "her age, the nature and length of her employment, and the composition of the family." If a woman had two or three children, she was a "preferred candidate" for the loan, since she was less likely to have more children.

If the wife were young and the couple persistent about seeking a mortgage, then the VA might inquire as to birth control practices. The VA explained:

In certain instances, a veteran and his wife may be unable to have children and supporting medical evidence may be submitted to the lender for transmittal to the VA to establish the likelihood of the wife continuing to work. If such a medical statement is voluntarily submitted by the veteran to the lender, it cannot very well be refused upon receipt in the VA.

This is the United States government speaking!

In one case, *United States* v. *Jefferson Mortgage Company*, filed under the Fair Housing Act just prior to the passage of the ECOA, a mortgage banker was accused of engaging in just such practices. The mortgage banker, who did most of his work with VA and FHA, asserted as a defense that he was only pursuing VA policy and requirements. The case was settled with a consent decree.

No wonder a Virginia bank could get away with requiring a wife who wanted to count her income on a mortgage to sign papers agreeing to an abortion if she were to become pregnant during the life of the loan. Ironically, such a lender was probably so conservative that he would ordinarily have opposed abortion. How appalling and ridiculous our credit situation was!

Failure to count the wife's income meant that many medium-income couples were denied the benefits of home ownership. Can you picture what would happen to the housing market today if lenders tried to follow these rules?

Such serious invasions of personal privacy were not in the Middle Ages! The year was 1973.

5. DIVORCED OR WIDOWED WOMEN

The wife who used her husband's first name had no identity of her own in the credit community, as many women learned after a change in marital status. It was during these crisis periods that a woman was least likely to be able to obtain credit as a "new applicant." Creditors looked at new as "new" regardless of the fact that she had managed the family accounts for years.

Senator Brock received letters from many women who had been separated, deserted, divorced, or widowed, who found that bereavement or separation was compounded by a loss of identity in the financial community. Women whose income had sufficed to secure their families' credit in the past suddenly found that the same means counted for nothing.

One divorced woman who had enjoyed credit for several years was asked by a department store to reapply for credit after her account had been closed when she notified the store of her court order restoring her maiden name. Since divorced men don't change their names, the stores usually had no way even to know when men divorced, and certainly didn't cancel their credit! Even after working wives had departed with their earnings, divorced men continued to enjoy the benefits of a family credit rating built up over the years with the assistance of their wives' incomes.

One of many letters I found in the National Organization for Women (NOW) files described this annoying, frustrating, and sometimes devastating discrimination:

> I separated four years ago. My income from my job and child support was not great, but was certainly well above the poverty level. I was immediately turned down for credit by Sears, Roebuck and Company, MasterCharge and BankAmericard. So I then lied in order to maintain the charge account we had had for years at Lansburghs. I merely changed it to my name without giving my change in status. The others gave me no reason, just a form letter. Last year, with a much better income, I again applied at Sears, Roebuck and Company and also at Esso and Bank-Americard. I received a form letter turning me down from BankAmericard, never heard from Esso, and received a letter requesting an interview from Sears. I had always paid my bills promptly and resented having to go for a personal interview. But I went and after some hassling with the credit manager, got my credit card.
>
> I had to laugh when, two weeks ago, I received a letter from Sears bemoaning the fact that I haven't used my charge account in a long time and giving me a $5.00 gift certificate if I would only come in and charge $25.00 worth of goods.

Here's another typical case concerning a Maryland professional woman who divorced her husband. At the time of their separation, she and her husband were earning comparable incomes and shared the financial responsibility for a joint department store account. Upon divorce, the account was transferred to her husband's name alone, without his reapplying, whereas she had to reapply and open a new account.

Understandably, after sorting through all these horror stories, about this time I started worrying about how my own credit rating looked. A note on my calendar reminded me to "check my credit rating" and "get credit cards, MasterCharge and BankAmericard by myself."

After almost three months of researching, memo writing, and "politicking," in early April, Bill Brock told me to move ahead on getting the bill ready for introduction. In the next few days, the senator prepared his remarks for inclusion when he introduced the legislation on April 17.

From after Easter recess to the passage of the legislation in the Senate, my life was focused on it. As we moved toward the Banking Committee consideration of the bill in late June, several main issues emerged. They included questions about the need to include the phrase "marital status"; the role of the Equal Credit Opportunity Act in community property states; whether race and other factors would be included; and what the penalties would be for violation, including class action provisions so that members of an affected group could sue together.

Marital status became a big issue because it cut to the core of the problem. Much of women's economic inequality arises within the context of marriage and family roles, the legal definition of which goes back to the early Middle Ages.

In his commentaries on English Common Law, from which our own separate property states took their cue, a British judge in the 1700s, Sir William Blackstone, set forth the principle this way:

By marriage, the husband and wife are one person in law: That is, the very being or legal existence of the woman is suspended during the marriage, or at least is incorporated and consolidated into that of her husband.

Notice: The "very being" of the woman was suspended.

These laws have since been updated by the passage of married women's property acts, but not surprisingly, as we will soon see, women experience continuing marital status credit problems today.

Congress recognized that "there is a subtle line of distinction between discrimination on the basis of sex and discrimination on the basis of marital status." Not only do married women experience discrimination, unmarried people of both sexes face difficulties as well. For example, two unmarried people of either sex were often prevented from buying a home together.

Much of the opposition on the marital status issue came from senators from community property states, for at the time the law was being enacted several of these states did not allow women much control over the community property in which they held a 50 percent interest.

To do these senators justice, there would have been some conflicts between the intent of the Equal Credit Opportunity Act and their own state laws. On this point Senator Brock stood particularly firm. If the Equal Credit Opportunity Act conflicted with these laws, then the laws ought to be preempted under the constitutional rules giving Congress the right to regulate interstate commerce. In the end, the law contained some compromises around community property, but justice was served anyway, for most of the states modified their laws in response to the changing times, of which the Equal Credit Opportunity Act was one signal.

The issue of mortgage credit discrimination was closely tied to race, but sex discrimination in mortgages wasn't so well known. Mortgage lenders directly, or in practice, "drew lines" around minority areas—a practice known as redlining—and would not give credit to persons living in those areas on the same terms as credit was available to others. The result was recognized as discriminatory. Sex discrimination in housing and mortgage credit was equally debilitating and much more open and direct—but it was socially and legally acceptable. Mortgage credit discrimination—what I called "pinklining"—kept women from buying homes on their own. Rather than outlawing sex discrimination in housing, the federal government legitimized discrimination against women through its own agency guidelines, as we saw above.

To make sure we had plenty of protection on mortgage credit, Senator Brock decided to sponsor an amendment to the Fair Housing Act—the one responsible for the sign in the bank—to add that missing term: sex. Because of the pattern that had been established in the other civil rights legislation in 1972, when the employment and education acts were amended to add sex, we did not include marital status. Since the Fair Housing Act or Title VIII was part of this large body of law, it was felt that the same language should apply.

As for race discrimination in credit other than mortgage credit, after some discussion it was decided not to include it in the original version of the Equal Credit Opportunity Act. The reasoning was twofold. The main reason was based on the evidence presented in 1972 by the National Commission on Consumer Finance, which couldn't find clear-cut proof of racial discrimination other than for mortgage credit. Second, without this clear evidence, Banking Committee supporters of the legislation thought the addition of race would weaken support for the bill since attention would be diverted to discussing race discrimination in mortgage credit, which was already covered in the Fair Housing Act.

Ordinarily, business credit has not been covered under the

consumer credit protection laws, but because of its importance to women in gaining their economic rights, Senator Brock included it. Before final passage, this section was watered down in the marital status provisions' coverage, but the spirit remained.

Damage provisions for violations put the financial teeth into a law. On this question, Senator Brock held the view that social legislation need not lead to excessive litigation in order to be effective. Therefore, the damage provisions of the law as he introduced them and as they ultimately passed were less favorable than many women wished. But Senator Brock felt that the law, as passed, did provide sufficient penalties to protect women.

In addition to the substantive issues surrounding the Equal Credit Opportunity Act and the Fair Housing Act amendment, the political process itself required attention. Senator Proxmire, chairman of the Banking Committee, had his own goals. Also, Senator Harrison Williams had introduced a credit bill in response to a constituent complaint, and his contribution had to be included. Finally, Bella Abzug's bills were still before the House and other members slowly started "cosponsoring" them or introducing their own versions.

If success were to be achieved, all the different interests had to be coalesced, so I kept up my routine of keeping in touch. Senator Williams joined Brock's bill. Later Senator Proxmire came on board. We also started signing up other senators as cosponsors.

As for players outside Congress, one of my roles was to help gain support from the women's movement for Brock's efforts. First I often felt isolated. I had landed in the middle of the Washington women's establishment as an outsider from California, so I wasn't known personally to many of the women, and Senator Brock had a conservative image that many feminists initially mistrusted. Soon I met other women who had been working by themselves on the issue and they welcomed my enthusiasm.

Before the issue reached the floor of the Senate, the leaders of the National Organization for Women (NOW), the National Women's Political Caucus (NWPC), the Women's Lobby, the Women's Equity Action League (WEAL), and other women's groups all became friends and allies.

People like Sharyn Campbell, NOW's credit task force chair, who had worked hard on her project before I came to Washington, began to help me. Eric Hirschhorn and Marilyn Magnusson from Bella Abzug's staff pitched in. The Center for Women's Policy Study founders, Marge Gates and Jane Chapman, lent me their earlier study on credit. Carol Burris of the Women's Lobby, Jane McMichael of the NWPC, Ellen Sudow of the Congressional Democratic Study, and Patricia Massey from WEAL all appeared frequently on my call list. Two key people through all of this were Ken McLean, who was then Chairman William Proxmire's chief staffer on the Banking Committee, and Paul Skrabut from Senator Harrison Williams's office.

My calendar for the next few months was filled with calls back and forth around Washington and the country. The next year, during final passage, many other people got involved, but in this first year, 1973, there were only a handful of us working regularly on the Equal Credit Opportunity Act.

On the other side of the political fence, the American Bankers' Association and several government agencies were still putting up resistance. No one said outright, "We don't want women to have equal credit," but they mustered seemingly logical, rational, and legalistic arguments to resist change.

Despite all, the bill got through Committee and as the "staffer" responsible, I was now asked by the committee to draft its report for the full Senate's review.

During my months of research, I had found credit problems that the original National Commission on Consumer Finance had not discovered, so we added this list to the examples of discriminatory practices for the committee report. Many of the items on this list were later reflected in Regulation B when it finally took effect in 1977.

In June 1973, the committee's list of discriminatory practices included:

1. Holding women and men to different standards in determining creditworthiness—for example, minimum salary level (without regard to individual obligations), length of employment, length of residence, and so forth.

2. Requiring a newly married woman whose creditworthiness has otherwise remained the same to reapply for credit as a new applicant.

3. Refusing to extend credit to a married woman in her own name, even though she would be deemed creditworthy if unmarried.

4. Refusing to count a wife's income or discounting it when a married couple applies for credit, including jointly held credit cards or accounts, secured or unsecured loans, and mortgage loans.

5. Refusing to extend credit to a newly separated or divorced woman solely because of her change in marital status.

6. Arbitrary refusal to consider alimony and child support as a valid source of income where such source is subject to verification.

7. Applying stricter standards in the case of married applicants where the wife rather than the husband is the primary family supporter.

8. Requesting or using information about birth control practices in evaluating any credit application.

9. Requesting or using information concerning the creditworthiness of a spouse where an otherwise creditworthy married person applies for credit as an individual.
10. Refusing to issue separate accounts to married persons where each would be creditworthy if unmarried.
11. Considering as "dependents" spouses who are employed and not actually dependent on the applicant.
12. Use of credit scoring systems that apply different values depending on sex or marital status.
13. Altering an individual's credit rating on the basis of the credit rating of the spouse.

After the committee reported the bill, barely a month remained before it was to go to the full United States Senate. In that month, our focus shifted to ensuring that we had strong support for the legislation when it reached the floor so that the bill would pass without being weakened.

Finally the day arrived. On the floor of the Senate on July 23, 1973, I was standing by with backup arguments prepared in case of last-minute opposition. As the minutes ticked by, it became clear that the months of work had paid off. On that historic day no one was willing to go on record as against credit equality for women. The bill passed 90–0.

After Senate passage, my time was heavily taken up with meeting members of Congress and their staffs on behalf of Senator Brock to explain the bill and to consolidate support for it in the House. About this time, the Nixon White House decided to get involved as well. Senator Brock met with the White House and Justice Department representatives and soon the administration decided to support the Brock version.

On the House side, sponsorship for the legislation grew rapidly. Many members introduced versions of the act just passed in the Senate. Congresswoman Margaret Heckler (R-

Massachusetts) took a leading role and Congresswoman Bella Abzug (D-New York) continued her leadership. Congresswoman Yvonne Brathwaite Burke (D-California) and Congresswoman Patricia Schroeder (D-Colorado) became early supporters, as well as Congressman Fortney ("Pete") Stark (D-California) and Congressman Matthew Rinaldo (R-New Jersey).

Ironically, the Banking Subcommittee on the House side, which had to hear the legislation, was headed by the only woman member of Congress, Leonore Sullivan, who did not want to support the legislation. As the summer turned to fall, pressure was mounting, but it took another year of hearings, politics, and compromise before the Equal Credit Opportunity Act became law.

At this stage, many new people became involved in passage of the act. Major long-standing women's groups such as the American Association of University Women and the Federation of Business and Professional Women, and other groups such as Consumer Federation, joined those already active. Congressman Ed Koch (D-New York) played a key role in getting congressional hearings set. These historical roles have been discussed in the references cited in Appendix 1 to this book.

In the meanwhile, I had finished my main contribution, having helped achieve Senate passage, and I returned to California to campaign for Congress myself.

On October 28, 1974, the final act was passed. The law prohibiting discrimination in granting credit on the basis of sex or marital status went into effect a year later. The amendment to the Fair Housing Act, adding sex, went into effect at the same time.

Although the final passage of the act in 1974 is now rightly viewed as one of the success stories of the women's movement, as Congress had opened in 1973, many Equal Rights Amendment (ERA) supporters fresh from their congressional victory of 1972 thought state ratification would soon be achieved, thus alleviating credit problems without the need for additional legislation. (Ironically opponents of ERA used the same argument against introduction of the legislation.)

Many people eventually worked for successful passage, but in the critical year of 1973 before a wider array of groups became involved, Senator Brock had the insight to recognize that credit for women was long overdue and the foresight to become committed when he did.

Exercise

YOUR CREDIT EXPERIENCES

1. Have you ever experienced any of the discriminatory practices discussed in this chapter?

2. If so, where, when?

3. What do you think the effect would have been had the Equal Credit Opportunity Act not passed?

Part Two

YOUR LEGAL RIGHTS

3

What the Law Provides and How It Works

The Equal Credit Opportunity Act establishes and protects women's access to credit. To eliminate discrimination it was necessary to make the credit system more open and consistent in its dealings, and this change has benefited all consumers. The law requires potential creditors to consider the credit applications of both women and men alike in certain prescribed ways. Just to take one example, anyone who applies for credit now has a legal right to an answer within thirty days of the fully completed application. This rule prohibits one practice through which creditors formerly avoided granting credit to women applicants—they simply failed to answer their credit requests. The thirty-day requirement helps us all, since when credit is involved, time is frequently of the essence.

The basic antidiscrimination provisions of the law address the twin issues of sex and marital status. In 1976, Congress strengthened the act to outlaw credit discrimination by race, color, religion, national origin, and age. While we will examine race and age discrimination in the credit system to some extent, our primary focus here is on the two factors that most apply to women across the board. Credit granting always involves choice on the part of the creditor. The point is those choices should be made without reference to gender or marital status.

Because our credit system was built before women joined it, there are biases in the system against women, particularly married women. The assumption still is that in a marriage, the man will have the final say over the money. Even professional women who are the primary family earners encounter this pitfall. For protection, you'll want to be sure, if married, to keep your credit identity separate. And, if you're unmarried, you'll want to be on guard against residual discriminatory habits of the system.

The best way to protect yourself is to know the law. In this chapter we'll look in detail at the Equal Credit Opportunity Act and Regulation B of the Board of Governors of the Federal Reserve System, which implements the law in specific detail.

CREDITORS COVERED BY THE EQUAL CREDIT OPPORTUNITY ACT

1. Which creditors are covered by the Equal Credit Opportunity Act?

- Banks and savings and loan companies
- Mortgage lenders (also Title VIII, the Fair Housing Act, covers mortgages for sex discrimination)
- Credit card issuers, including:
  Bank cards (Visa, MasterCard)
  Retailers (Sears, Montgomery Ward)

Oil companies

Travel and entertainment cards

- Sales finance companies (GMAC, Westinghouse Credit Corp.)
- Loan companies
- Consumer leasing companies
- Anyone else who regularly permits applicants to receive money, goods, or services, and defer payment, or participates in the decision to extend credit

2. Who isn't covered?

- Issuers of check cashing cards (unless linked to credit rating)
- People or businesses who don't regularly extend credit (e.g., your Uncle Harry)

3. These creditors are covered, but special exceptions apply:

- Public utility companies (telephone company, electric company)
- Arrangers of credit (real estate brokers, car dealers)
- Companies extending credit for business, commercial, or agricultural purposes
- Incidental creditors (no credit card involved, no finance charge, four or fewer installments—e.g., doctors, medical centers, some small merchants)
- Certain federal or state agencies (Federal Housing Administration, Small Business Administration, Veterans Administration)

While reading this chapter and the next two, note the numbers in parentheses by major points. These numbers refer to items in the tables at the end of the chapters. I developed these to give you a chance to look at the text of the law itself right along with examples, so if you encounter a problem, you'll be sufficiently conversant to quote the law! (If you are a person who finds footnotes distracting, read through the text of the chapter, then turn to the table.)

First, let's look at sex discrimination as covered in the law. Simply put, sex discrimination is treating women differently from men. (1) Since discrimination can take many forms, the law adds some specifics. Let's look at the ones you might encounter in your credit travels.

Although creditors cannot legally discourage women (or anyone else covered under the law) from applying, watch out. You may be discouraged without your realizing it. The loan officer who "helpfully" steers you away from applying because you might be turned down and says it will "look bad on your record" may be more worried about *his* record. The federal agencies that oversee the credit laws monitor performance on credit granting. If you are marginally qualified and don't apply, then you can't be compared to marginally qualified men, who often get the credit. (2)

Of course, you don't want too many "inquiries" on your credit report, but your record doesn't show rejections per se. Submit your application if you want the credit. If you don't apply, you certainly won't get it. (3)

Once you apply, you have the right to know within thirty days whether your application was accepted or rejected. (4) Here's what can happen, as a woman who wanted a student loan found out.

Weeks before, she had applied to Chase Manhattan Bank and was frantic since graduate school started in a few days. I suggested she send a mailgram citing the thirty-day requirement of the law. A few days later, her loan came through and she left for graduate school.

What if you apply and the answer is no? You must either

54

be told why or told that you have a right to know why. But there's a catch. If the creditor doesn't volunteer the reason for the rejection, you must ask within sixty days or forever hold your peace. The creditor then has thirty days to answer your request. (5)

Even though the specifics can be painful, if you're rejected, you'll want to know why. Perhaps there was a mistake and you can correct the error. Even if the information is right, you'll benefit. For example, if you were turned down for "too short a residence," you'll know how long to wait to reapply.

Remember, the law spells out acceptable reasons that can be given for an "adverse action." For example, a creditor cannot simply tell you that you "failed on a credit scoring system"; instead, a more exact reason, such as "length of employment," must be given. (6)

Being told that "length of employment" was the reason for rejection is even generally unhelpful, since a person cannot do anything to affect the length of employment other than sit and wait. Also, there may be no "magic number" for an acceptable length of employment. That reason is given simply because a person lost the most points on that characteristic in a credit scoring system.

The law doesn't require the creditor to tell you how much longer you need to hold a job or the length of residence you need, but by asking you can often obtain this information. If the time differences are short, you may want to "sit and wait" to reapply. Also, if an account is canceled because of inactivity or delinquency, this is not counted as an "adverse action" under the Equal Credit Opportunity Act and the creditor is not obligated to explain, although the creditor could report the cancellation to a credit reporting agency and it would appear on your record.

But what if you apply for credit and instead of telling you no, the creditor gives you less credit than you needed? Let's say you applied for a Visa card with a limit of $1,000 and you were given one with $250. Or, let's say you had credit somewhere and suddenly your account was canceled. The same applies—you must be told why or told that you have the right to ask why. (7)

Let's look at how one irate consumer handled a "No." A secretary with the same company five years, Jean Smithson applied for a J. C. Penney's card. According to her application, Smithson earned $1,550 per month and her major fixed commitment was monthly rent of $375. With two paid-up accounts and one credit union account at her employer's, her debt load appeared well within prescribed limits of 25 percent toward rent plus other debts not over an additional 20 percent.

J. C. Penney's reply followed the law by telling Ms. Smithson she had a right to know why she was refused, and Ms. Smithson wrote back as required, to ask why.

Penney's second response pointed to Ms. Smithson's failure to obtain the minimum score required to qualify for an account. They listed the factors that affected their decision, which included years at address, type of occupation, and length of time on job.

Penney's complied completely with the law, but Ms. Smithson's case raises some interesting questions. Credit scoring systems are perfectly legal as long as they are based on statistically sound criteria. (8) In nonhousing credit, credit scoring systems are the predominant type of credit decision-making tool. But these systems are secret, so there's no way for a consumer to judge their accuracy. And, because they are frequently built on assumptions and data bases compiled before women entered the credit system in large numbers, they fail to reflect accurately how women's life patterns differ from those of men.

Scoring systems are typically heavily weighted toward longevity in one job. How many otherwise creditworthy women are disqualified because they chose to raise a family and then return to the workplace? What happens to a recently divorced woman who has moved and obtained a new job? And what about all the women whose occupations are not valued by the system?

While most overt forms of sex discrimination in credit were ended by the Equal Credit Opportunity Act (no banker these days will come out and tell a consumer she's being refused credit because she is a woman), credit scoring systems and less rigorous "judgmental" systems continue to give women problems and may well fail the "effects test," a legal concept that says, "an action may be deemed discriminatory if the effect is discriminatory even though on its face the policy is sexually neutral."

Yet, how can consumers legally challenge these systems if they are secret? (See chapter 6 for more on credit scoring systems.)

At least one component of scoring systems was definitely changed by the law. If a creditor ever asks you if you have a phone listing in your name, tell him that's illegal! It's okay for a creditor to count whether you have a telephone, but he can't force you to publicly list the number to qualify for credit. (9) Creditors assign a considerable value to the phone as an instrument of collection. Before the Equal Credit Opportunity Act, creditors frequently gave high marks for a listed phone number. Since women often prefer to avoid sexual harassment by not listing their numbers or by putting them in their husbands' names, lack of a phone listing often was enough to disqualify an otherwise creditworthy woman.

Even though by 1972 a third of women with children under six worked, creditors ("B.C.," Before Credit) assumed that the future possibility of motherhood rendered women unfit for credit. For men, almost the opposite view held: The "little dears" would tie him down to regular habits, including regular bill paying.

The Equal Credit Opportunity Act makes this feudalistic concern with fertility absolutely illegal. Don't let anyone go on a fishing expedition with you. A proper inquiry into the number of dependents you have can quickly become an illegal foray into your child-bearing plans. Don't let it. (10)

Because of motherhood or the requirements of homemaking, women often opt for part-time employment. Again, before the credit law, rather than rewarding women for choosing this traditional path, the system penalized them. Creditors are now prohibited from discounting or refusing to consider income because it is derived from part-time employment. (11)

If you've been previously married and now rely on alimony, creditors must give full weight to your income, even if it's solely alimony or child support. As long as you're otherwise qualified for the credit you seek and you can show your income is regular, they're as good as any other source of funds. (12) However, a creditor has the right to determine the likelihood the alimony/child support income will continue, and therefore may inquire about the ex-spouse's credit and, under appropriate circumstances, discount it (when the income is irregular). However, it is clear that such income cannot be disregarded out of hand.

Lawmakers also added pension, annuity, or retirement income. Since so many women outlive men and find themselves dependent upon these sources of support, this provision is of special help to women. (13) Discrimination against age after sixty-two is also prohibited, which especially benefits older women. (14) Before age sixty-two age can be used as a factor if based on a sound statistical basis.

Yet as one Massachusetts woman learned, creditors don't always comply with the law. A widow from Natick with a total of $950 per month in disability, annuity, and social security income couldn't persuade creditors to count her income. If this widow had wanted a thirty-year mortgage, her longevity might have been a valid issue, but she simply wanted a Visa card to purchase theater tickets by telephone.

Another key area covered by the act, racial discrimination (other than mortgage credit) eludes easy proof, as we saw in chapter 2. Yet when I get a letter like this one from Virginia, I can't help wondering what, other than racial discrimination, could cause her inability to obtain credit, compounded, as it is in this case, by possible sex discrimination.

I am writing this letter, hoping that you will be able to give me advice on establishing credit. I am a twenty-nine-year-old Black female, and have been applying for credit for eight years and have not been able to obtain it.

What baffles me the most, I guess, is that a college student with no steady income can get credit cards without even asking for them!!! They are sent applications in the mail and the company might ask for a cosigner but nine times out of ten, not even that. I have been working steadily for nine years and the last five, I've spent with the federal government. I'm making approximately $18,000, which is a major criteria for obtaining a credit card with Visa, MasterCard, or American Express. I've just purchased my second car—the first, financed by Service Federal Credit Union, the other Chrysler Credit Corporation. If I can purchase cars on credit and pay them off in good standing, why can't I get a retail credit card???

This writer enclosed proof of her good credit performance and a copy of a clean credit record. Here's a person who surely is qualified for a bank card.

In a Chinese restaurant in New York, I saw a sign posted by the cash register that further confirms my suspicions that creditors think in racial stereotypes. A major credit card company, in an attempt to prevent fraud, sent an instructive notice depicting typical problem situations. One item featured a card in the name of "Catherine Frost." Beside the card, the following scenario appears: "It's September 1982 . . . A person of definite Hispanic origin, complete with an accent, wants to check into your hotel."

The cashier is then warned not to take the card because, "The Anglo name on the card does not correspond with the physical description of the card presenter."

The possibility that a Spanish-speaking woman named Catherine might marry Mr. Frost has evidently never crossed the minds of this company's policymakers. No wonder women of color still encounter credit barriers. (15)

Table 2. THE EQUAL CREDIT OPPORTUNITY ACT AND REGULATION B— SEX, AGE, AND RACE DISCRIMINATION

Problem 1*
Being treated differently because you are a woman.

Example: An attorney is turned down for a credit card and her husband, a doctor, who earns less and shares the same credit record, is approved for the same card.

Solution: General tips for dealing with a case of sex discrimination: Write a letter, return receipt requested, to the head of customer relations with a copy to the president of the company, general counsel of the company, the Federal Trade Commission (FTC), and the Department of Justice. The copy lines should be showing on the letter. The letter should be temperate and simply lay out the facts and the reasons why the rejection of credit was inappropriate. Include additional credit

*Keyed to numbers in text, chapters 3, 4, and 5.

facts which you believe may not be known to the company. Always keep a copy of every piece of paper that you submit to the company.

Obtain the names of the persons whom you deal with over the telephone and in person. Write down their names and the time and day on which you spoke with them. Keep your notes.

Obtain a copy of your credit report. If the credit report contains inaccurate information or incomplete information, write a letter to the credit reporting company correcting it and send a copy of the letter to the source that provided the incorrect information. Request strongly that correct information be provided. Send a copy of these letters to the creditor with whom you are dealing.

Submit independent proof of your earnings or job longevity, particularly if these are very strong assets.

If turned down for credit, always get the reasons. You must request in writing that specific reasons be sent to you.

The Law: The key operational paragraphs of the Equal Credit Opportunity Act [Public Law 93-495, Sect. 701]:

"701. Prohibited discrimination; reasons for adverse action

"(a) It shall be unlawful for any creditor to discriminate against any applicant, with respect to any aspect of a credit transaction—

"(1) on the basis of race, color, religion, national origin, sex or marital status, or age (provided the applicant has the capacity to contract)."

Key definitions in the law:

- "The term 'applicant' means any person who applies to a creditor directly for an extension, renewal, or continuation of credit, or applies to a creditor indirectly by use of an existing credit plan for an amount exceeding a previously established credit limit." [Sect. 702(b).]
- "The term 'credit' means the right granted by a creditor to a debtor to defer payment of debt or to incur debt and defer its payment or to purchase property or services and defer payment thereof." [Sect. 702(d).]
- "The term 'creditor' means any person who regularly extends,

renews, or continues credit; any person who regularly arranges for the extension, renewal, or continuation of credit; or any assignee of an original creditor who participates in the decision to extend, renew, or continue credit." [Sect. 702(e).] Certain creditors have special provisions. (See no. 25, chapter 4.)

Problem 2
How to ensure creditors were complying with the law.

Example: A young woman applies for an auto loan and is rejected. Later she learns that a male co-worker who earns less is accepted by the same bank for a similarly priced car. She writes to the FTC to report her concern.

But note that the FTC rarely responds on a one-on-one basis. The most profitable route to getting credit is often "self-help" through correspondence with the creditor, bringing your concerns to its attention.

Solution: The law requires record retention for federal monitoring purposes. If you apply (the application has to be completed to be counted), the creditor must keep the application for 25 months. In our case here, a federal agency chooses whether to see the records, based on current policy, but if they don't follow through on individual cases, you can challenge a decision with an attorney, who could then get access to the necessary information.

The Law: "For 25 months after the date that a creditor notifies an applicant of action taken on an application, the creditor shall retain . . . that application in original form or a copy thereof." [Regulation B, Sect. 202.12(b).]

Problem 3
Women and minorities discouraged from applying.

Example: A woman goes in to apply and is told that she probably won't qualify, so there's no point in applying.

Solution: Take an application and apply. Ask for policies.

The Law: The language of Regulation B states:

"A creditor shall not make any oral or written statement in advertising or otherwise, to applicants or prospective applicants that would discourage . . . a reasonable person from making or pursuing an application." [Regulation B, Sect. 202.5(a).]

Problem 4

Women apply for credit but no answer given.

Example: A woman mails in an application in a women's magazine for a Visa card. Two months later she hasn't heard anything.

Solution: Photocopy and date all applications mailed. If no response within the required 30 days, send a copy to the attention of some person in the organization who deals with snafus with a reminder that the Equal Credit Opportunity Act requires a response to a completed application in 30 days. Remember, the clock doesn't start until the creditor has all the information about you, including your credit report.

The Law: The language of the ECOA is:

"Within thirty days . . . after receipt of a completed application for credit, a creditor shall notify the applicant of its action on the application." [Sect. 701(d) (1).]

Problem 5

Turned down but no reason given.

Example: A woman applies for a department store card and receives a letter that says "your application has been reviewed and we have not been able to approve it."

Solution: Write and ask for specific reasons for being turned down. You must write within 60 days. You should be aware that the case law has developed here more clearly than in any other areas of ECOA. The creditor must give reasons and must give accurate, complete, and specific reasons. An answer of the kind cited in the example would be actionable and would give the applicant some leverage in dealing with the institution.

The Law: The specific language about adverse action and statement of reasons is:

"Each applicant against whom adverse action is taken shall be entitled to a statement of reasons for such action from the creditor." [Sect. 701(d) (2).]

Problem 6

Creditors traditionally gave no reason for denying credit, or gave flimsy excuses.

Example: A woman applies for a department store card and is rejected. When she calls to ask why, she is told "you don't meet our standards." She then writes in and the reply is "you do not meet the qualifying score on our credit scoring system."

Solution: The creditor must give actual reasons, not general ones. The reasons in the example are too general.

You should know that the principal reasons listed under the law are taken from the model form provided by the Federal Reserve Board. The courts have held that this form does not provide iron-clad protection to a creditor. The creditor's reason must be very specific and accurate, and the use of a "boiler-plate" reason from the Federal Reserve list will not be adequate if it varies from the reasons actually used. The point of the solution here is for you to be prepared and willing to demonstrate the inaccuracy of the reason given based on the facts, even if the reason is on the list given here.

The Law: The principal reasons for adverse action concerning credit are:

> "Credit application incomplete.
> Insufficient credit references.
> Unable to verify credit references
> Temporary or irregular employment
> Unable to verify employment
> Length of employment
> Insufficient income
> Excessive obligations

Unable to verify income
Inadequate collateral
Too short a period of residence
Temporary residence
Unable to verify residence
No credit file
Insufficient credit file
Delinquent credit obligations
Garnishment, attachment, foreclosure,
    repossession, or suit
Bankruptcy
We do not grant credit to any applicant on
    the terms and conditions you request
Other, specify:"

[Regulation B, Sect. 202.9(b) (2).]

Problem 7

An account is revoked, a request for increased credit limit is denied, existing credit is not renewed.

Example: The card for an account, kept in good standing, expires, and no new card is issued. No explanation is given. When the consumer calls to find out why, she's told that she had not complied with company "policies."

Solution: The creditor has violated the law by not notifying the consumer of the "adverse action" and letting you know you have the right to specific reasons. Request, in writing, the reason for the action.

It is not adverse action for the use of a credit card to be denied at the point of sale.

The Law: The law spells out exactly what constitutes an "adverse action."

"For purposes of this subsection, the term 'adverse action' means a denial or revocation of credit, a change in the terms of an existing credit arrangement, or a refusal to grant credit in substantially the amount or on substantially the terms requested. Such term does not include a refusal to extend additional credit under an existing credit arrangement where the applicant is delinquent or otherwise in default, or where such additional credit would exceed a previously established credit limit." [Sect. 701(d) (6).]

Problem 8
A credit scoring system disqualifies a consumer.

Example: A woman lived in the same home for 15 years, but bought a new condo two months ago. She applies for a department store account in her new neighborhood, but is denied credit because she is "not long enough in her residence."

Solution: This example is just one of the characteristics of credit scoring systems that creditors claim mathematically predict creditworthiness. Two solutions are: (a) Ask what would correct the situation under the system; (b) Meet with the decision-maker and show how the system is not a good predictor in your case.

Consumers do have the ability to apply pressure to the creditor to disclose more information about the combination of variables that predicted the rejection and the reason that this particular variable was chosen for disclosure.

The Law: Credit scoring systems are allowed under the Equal Credit Opportunity Act, and Regulation B spells out the details. The allowable purpose of these systems is for:
"Predicting the creditworthiness of applicants with respect to the legitimate business interests of the creditor utilizing the system, including, but not limited to, minimizing bad debt losses and operating expenses in accordance with the creditor's business judgment." [Regulation B, Section 202.2(p) (2) (ii).]
The key requirement for these systems is that they:
"Upon validation using appropriate statistical principles, separate creditworthy and noncreditworthy applicants at a statistically significant rate." [Regulation B, Sect. 202.2(p) (2) (iii).]

Problem 9
An application for credit asks: Do you have a telephone in your name?

Example: A widow has kept her phone listing in her husband's name in the ten years since he died. When she applies for credit, she's told: "You have to have a phone listed in your name."

Solution: The law says a creditor can't require a phone to be listed in a person's name, only that there be a phone in the home. Tell the creditor that this is a clear violation of Regulation B! (Also, it would be a good idea to change the phone to your name and list it by first initial. Otherwise, if you ever move, you'll have to pay a deposit because you have no personal utility track record.)

The Law: Regulation B took care of the telephone problem by stating:
"A creditor shall not take into account the existence of a telephone listing in the name of an applicant for consumer credit. A creditor may take into account the existence of a telephone in the residence of such an applicant." [Regulation B, Sect. 202.6(b) (4).]

Problem 10
It has been assumed that women will have children, stay home and default on their debts.

Example: A young pregnant woman wants to count her income as the prime earner for a mortgage. The lender is worried that she might change her mind, and want to stay home when the baby comes—and tells her so.

Solution: It is illegal to assume that you will drop out of the work force just because you plan to have children. Point out that not only are such considerations illegal, but that you'd hardly want to undertake an obligation only to default a few months later.

The Law: Regulation B, carrying out the specific intent of Congress not to penalize mothers and would-be mothers, provides:
"A creditor shall not request information about birth control practices, intentions concerning the bearing or rearing of children, or capability to bear children. This does not preclude a creditor from inquiring about the number and ages of an applicant's dependents or about dependent-related financial obligations or expenditures, provided such

67

information is requested without regard to sex, marital status, or any other prohibited basis." [Regulation B, Sect. 202.5(d) (4).]

To make the case clear, creditors were reminded:

"A creditor shall not use, in evaluating the creditworthiness of an applicant, assumptions or aggregate statistics relating to the likelihood that any group of persons will bear or rear children or, for that reason, will receive diminished or interrupted income in the future." [Regulation B, Sect. 202.6(b) (3).]

Problem 11
Part-time income not counted.

Example: A woman earning $1,200 per month as a part-time secretary can't get credit because her income isn't "regular" even though she has steadily earned this much over the past four years.

Solution: Point out to the creditor that the law says part-time income must be counted. Creditors often tend to equate regular part-time work, which provides a reliable salary, with temporary work which may not.

The Law: "A creditor shall not discount or exclude from consideration the income of an applicant or the spouse of the applicant because of a prohibited basis or because the income is derived from part-time employment, or from an annuity, pension, or other retirement benefit; but a creditor may consider the amount and probable continuance of any income in evaluating an applicant's creditworthiness." [Regulation B, Sect. 202.6(b) (5).]

Problem 12
On one hand, creditors illegally use the fact of alimony to establish divorce, then turn around and refuse to count alimony as income.

Example: A divorced mother of three earns $1,500 a month, which is not enough to qualify for a car loan she wants. But with her child support she qualifies. She's not sure whether to report this income.

Solution: If you receive your child support or alimony regularly, by all means report it. But if you can't prove that you get it by demonstrating regular receipt or if it arrives irregularly, counting it won't help and may actually harm your chances because it contributes to an unsettled appearance. The quesiton of whether or not to disclose this income can be decided in the affirmative if you can go armed with receipts, check stubs, or a statement by the payor that would make it difficult for a creditor to discount the source of income.

The Law: "Where an applicant relies on alimony, child support, or separate maintenance payments in applying for credit, a creditor shall consider such payments as income to the extent that they are likely to be consistently made. Factors that a creditor may consider in determining the likelihood of consistent payments include . . . whether the payments are received pursuant to a written agreement or court decree; the length of time that the payments have been received; the regularity of receipt; the availability of procedures to compel payment; and the creditworthiness of the payor, including the credit history of the payor where available under the Fair Credit Reporting Act or other applicable laws." [Regulation B, Sect. 202.6(b) (5).]

Problem 13
Women and men on social security, disability, and welfare need credit, too.

Example: A retired schoolteacher receiving social security, disability, and a small pension wants a Visa or MasterCard but the bank will only count her pension, so she doesn't have enough income to qualify.

Solution: Remind the creditor that the law requires your income to be counted.

The Law: Creditors are also prohibited from discriminating in a credit transaction:
  "Because all or part of the applicant's income derives from any public assistance program." [Sect. 701(a) (2) and no. 5 above.]

Problem 14
Older persons denied credit on basis they won't "live long enough to pay it off."

Example: A 70-year-old widow wants a travel card to visit her children. Although not told directly, she suspects her age is a problem since her income is generous.

Solution: Remind the creditor that age discrimination is illegal, unless you actually couldn't pay the debt, e.g., in the case of a 30-year mortgage.

Elderly is defined for credit purposes as age 62. Ineligibility for credit life insurance is often a reason for age discrimination even though it is illegal to require insurance as a condition of getting credit. Short-term credit where life expectancy is not an issue should not be denied on the basis of age, and, in fact, the statistics indicate that older persons are better credit risks than younger persons.

The Law: "(i) Except as permitted in this subsection, a creditor shall not take into account an applicant's age (provided that the applicant has the capacity to enter into a binding contract) or whether an applicant's income derives from any public assistance program.

"(ii) In a demonstrably and statistically sound, empirically derived credit system, a creditor may use an applicant's age as a predictive variable, provided that the age of an elderly applicant is not assigned a negative factor or value.

"(iii) In a judgmental system of evaluating creditworthiness, a creditor may consider an applicant's age or whether an applicant's income derives from any public assistance program only for the purpose of determining a pertinent element of creditworthiness.

"(iv) In any system of evaluating creditworthiness, a creditor may consider the age of an elderly applicant when such age is to be used to favor the elderly applicant in extending credit." [Regulation B, Sect. 202.6(b) (2) (i–iv).]

Problem 15

Racial discrimination prevented many persons from obtaining credit.

Example: A young white couple goes to Hertz to rent a car in New York City. They don't have a credit card, but with a $300 cash deposit they get the car. A young black couple tries to do the same and is turned down. They're told, "Your credit wasn't approved."

Solution: Remind the rental company that the refusal to rent based on your credit falls under the Equal Credit Opportunity Act, according to a recent 9th Circuit Court of Appeals decision.

Ask specifically what was wrong with your credit, as provided in above, and suggest race discrimination.

The example cited is also a violation of the 1966 Civil Rights Act and probably a state and local law as well. It is a significantly more serious violation than, say, an improper adverse action notice.

The Law: "It shall be unlawful for any creditor to discriminate against any applicant, with respect to any aspect of a credit transaction, on the basis of race, color, religion, national origin, sex, or marital status, or age (provided the applicant has the capacity to contract)." [Sect. 701(a) (1).]

4

Married Women's Credit

Marriage may be blissful, but your credit situation, if you are a married woman, may not be. Once your financial identity has been tangled with a man's, it's hard to get it free!

Whether you are married or have been married, the mere presence of a man in your life can serve to change your credit standing despite a law to the contrary.

The continued credit discrimination against married women is a national problem of some magnitude. It has been partially obscured because married women often don't realize they don't have separate credit or because of the ease with which a married woman, if rejected, can decide, "Oh, well, I'll just use my husband's credit."

No matter how happily married you are, I recommend maintaining separate credit. Unfortunately, too many marriages today end in divorce. Also, most women outlive their spouses. If you don't want to face these facts—and who wouldn't rather ignore them—think about separate credit as a kind of "insurance." Hope you'll never need it, but have it for peace of mind.

Yet, many women put off getting credit. For one thing, even if women are convinced that they need separate credit, often their husbands aren't.

Perhaps you're like Lizzie Butler, a neighbor of my father's. When Lizzie heard I was writing a credit book, she invited me over for cookies, but soon the conversation turned to credit.

Lizzie and her retired husband, Bill, live comfortably in a pleasant home. They have savings and checking accounts, automobiles, and bank cards all in Bill's name. I advised Lizzie to ensure her own credit identity by getting credit on her own at once. All married women should do the same.

If this advice seems extreme, let me shake you out of your lethargy by sharing with you a letter I recently received from a widow.

When my husband was alive, I did not know about separate accounts. We had a credit account with Spiegels for almost thirty years, until he died in 1978. The account was in his name, but he got it for me to use.

I wrote to Spiegels last month to see if I could use them as a credit reference and they told me that the account was no longer active, so I was out of luck.

My husband never failed to pay. I think it is unfair to have an account in good standing for thirty years and not be able to use it as a credit reference.

Perhaps you're wondering what it is about marriage that makes a woman's situation so different. The answer lies in the legal history and is complicated by the fact that in our federal system two kinds of married property law coexist. Some states have separate property systems, deriving from English common law, and others have community property, deriving from the Spanish and French civil law.

The eight community property states are California, Texas, Arizona, New Mexico, Nevada, Louisiana, Idaho, and Washington. In 1984, Wisconsin became the first state to adopt the uniform Marital Property Act, a new nationally proposed standard that blurs the distinctions between the two and brings into Wisconsin marital law the general principles of community property law.

Under English common law, as we saw in chapter 2, married women lost their separate identity. A married woman was considered a suspended being, a person whose existence was subsumed by her husband. Among other privileges, she lost her capacity to contract. Even though by the nineteenth century separate control over earnings and the right to contract had been granted in most states by passage of married women's property acts, vestiges survived—guess where?—in the credit system! Bankers are said to be slow to change, but even so their tenacity in clinging to outmoded views on married women's property rights defies the imagination.

In community property law, it's assumed that husband and wife become an economic partnership, which helps women in many respects but has had a negative impact in gaining independent credit, partly because traditionally it was the husband, not the wife, who managed the unified whole.

Although here the laws have changed, even today, a decade after the passage of the Equal Credit Opportunity Act, married women are still experiencing difficulty. The situation is worse in community property states where some bankers seem bent on defying the law, even if it exposes them to the possibility of a lawsuit. As we saw in the Introduction, even as late as 1983, the largest bank in the nation, the Bank of America, had forms that illegally required spousal cosignature.

74

The differences among the state law systems in the treatment of marital property are reflected in the Equal Credit Opportunity Act. In separate property states, husbands' and wives' incomes are treated as their own, so for credit, marital status cannot be taken into account (16), nor can a cosignature be required for unsecured credit. (17)

In fact, in the separate property or common law states, creditors may not even ask your marital status, unless you're making a secured loan, which is treated differently because marriage creates certain rights to property for both spouses under both systems, rights that the Equal Credit Opportunity Act recognizes and protects. For secured credit, it's okay to get the spouse's signature on the security agreement, but not on the promissory note—so look for integrated notes that combine the two.

Under the act, creditors are allowed to ask marital status and the name of your spouse in the eight community property states. Since the community would be responsible for the debt, the creditor wants to know about that community. (18) But the creditor can't require a cosignature for credit.

In theory, a housewife should be able to commit the community—even if it's "his" earnings—on her signature alone if it is for unsecured credit. This area is controversial because a non-working wife theoretically is able to commit the earnings of the community, e.g., her spouse's earnings. In practice, creditors argue that future earnings of a spouse may not necessarily be available, so they are not technically community property, and thus cannot be committed by the non-earner until they are received.

One prominent industry spokesperson provided this argument: "Where is the logic in allowing a woman or man who earns zero to commit the $100,000 income of her or his spouse for a loan when the applicant does not or will not control

$100,000 upon divorce, separation, or movement out of state? The applicant is not asking to have their own property counted, but the future unearned income of another person. Insofar as this rule affects women, it should be pointed out that in most other states married women do not have this prerogative and cannot attempt to obtain an individual loan when they themselves have no income. (Of course the same applies for men.) Why should the idiosyncratic nature of community property law allow people to be treated differently under federal law in eight community property states than they are in the other states?" (19)

Creditors often choose to ignore the law, saying they are fighting it because they think it is wrong. So it's up to you to remind them. Until someone wins a really decisive case on this point, the practice of making a woman get her husband's signature—which translates to "asking his permission"—will continue, despite Congress's provision that the Equal Credit Opportunity Act should preempt state law and allow separate accounts if you are willing to be solely responsible. (20) This works for women who are credit-worthy, but for a housewife or a non-earner, it presents problems.

Again, in the community property states being solely responsible presents difficulties. The primary community property being committed is usually the earnings. If it is the wife who is unemployed, then it's the community earnings of the husband that are being committed. As we've seen, the wife has a right to commit the community, but there are two problems. First, some banks refuse to recognize future earnings, as compared with current income, as part of the community even though they have been told to do so by regulatory agencies who have reiterated that in a community property state, the credit decision for such an application turns on whether the applicant spouse has the legal power to bind the current and future income of the other spouse. Creditors maintain that future earnings are not community property and would not be available to the creditor in case of divorce. Many legal experts agree. Second, banks argue if there is a default on the obligation, it may be difficult for the creditor to sue the husband to recover the debt if the husband didn't sign the loan. Some consumer-oriented lawyers argue that the creditor can simply sue both spouses since the community was involved, but other experts note that under the UCC (Uniform Commercial Code) rules, to incur personal liability an individual must sign.

When we worked on the Equal Credit Opportunity Act in the U.S. Senate, many of these issues were raised, but it will take time through the courts to resolve them. For you, the consumer, the best course is to press for independent credit because, as we'll see, that's the only way a woman can ensure a continuing separate financial identity.

In both community property and separate property states, when property is involved, the rules change. In this case, usually a mortgage or a "promise to pay" secured by property is required. If a person defaults, a creditor wants to be able to sell the property to satisfy the unpaid debt. But marriage gives partners property rights, even when their names aren't on the title; therefore the Equal Credit Opportunity Act allows a creditor to ask for a spousal signature so the property will be properly pledged. (21)

But here again, creditors have stretched their rights and will often try to infringe on yours. Marital status *discrimination* is still illegal even when a marital status *inquiry* is allowed.

The creditor needs to ensure that the property is clear of other claims. To ensure a clear title, a creditor can ask for a quitclaim deed, in which a spouse says, "I don't claim to own this property." In addition, the creditor can get the spouse to sign the security agreement, or mortgage, which is different from the promissory note. Although both techniques will involve the spouse, thereby rendering completely independent action impossible, preserving the goal of property of your own in your own name with your own loan participation will ensure long-term financial independence so important to married women.

Of course, one-sided commitment can—and in the past did—work to the detriment of the wife. As one critic points out, "What is your reaction to the circumstance where the husband, also having full control of the community, goes out and commits the community to extensive debt for personal things such as cars and boats without disclosing this to the wife? Upon divorce the husband says let the wife pay for it equally with me since it was community property. Would you not argue in that circumstance that the wife has been victimized by the idiosyncracy of the law?"

The answer is "Yes—the wife would be victimized in this case, but usually lack of independence rather than profligate spending of one's spouse hurts most women in the end."

Often it's better to put both spouses on the loan and the title. Certainly neither you nor your husband would want to sign away your rights to the family home or major investments. But sometimes separate arrangements make more sense, and creditors will often cooperate.

The next best thing to having your own credit is to be sure credit you use is reported in your name as well as your spouse's. That way, you won't be a "Janie-come-lately" to the credit scene if you suddenly find yourself alone.

Your legal protection is excellent here. (22) All you have to do is request creditors to report all credits on which you are a user or for which you are liable in your name too. In community property states that would include all your spouse's credit since you'd be liable for it as well. Even when creditors don't ask for his co-signature on the credit application, they ask for it backhandedly by asking for his permission to obtain his credit report, as the Bank of America was doing. Although asking for cosignature of a loan is a gray area, asking for co-signature for a credit report is not. The creditor certainly has a right to see your spouse's credit report in a community property state, since both of you are liable for each other's debts as part of the community.

However, to look at your husband's credit report, all a creditor has to know is that you are liable, since by definition in community property states you would be liable for his debts. You have the right to ask the creditor to order his report without your husband's written permission.

If you meet resistance on this point, often made in the name of the privacy laws, point out that for most purposes under the provisions of the Fair Credit Reporting Act, a person has to agree in writing for his or her credit report to be released. But, under the Equal Credit Opportunity Act, which superseded the Fair Credit Reporting Act on this point, you can use your spouse's report for any account you use or for which you are liable. Your right of access is protected by Regulation B. In fact, I'd argue that in California and other community property states, credit bureaus are legally bound to transfer a complete spousal history, alleviating the necessity of creditor-by-creditor requests.

But legal protections don't work without consumer action. You must make the request for user reporting to the creditor, who has ninety days to comply, and you must double check by looking at your credit report. Resistant or slow creditors often drag their heels and may require prompting.

As for new accounts, every time you open one, make sure you check the box indicating you want the account reported in both names. Ask your husband to be sure to do this, too. You can build a credit identity even for accounts that are primarily used by your spouse, and he can get the benefit of your good credit by doing the same.

Of course, as you might suspect, all this togetherness has its drawback. If one or the other of you fall down, you'll both get the black mark. If you can demonstrate that you didn't use an account and were not responsible for delinquent payments, you can uncouple your credit, but that's not easy. (23)

If you're married to a man who doesn't pay his bills, consider getting rid of his name, at least for credit purposes. Put your credit in your birth name and keep it that way. It's legal! (24)

We've all heard of a woman who paid the family bills for years and then found herself alone without credit because all the credit was in her husband's name. Even though you should be able to get a creditor to look back at your spouse's history if you paid the bills, it's hard to get creditors to comply. An "ounce of prevention" works better. (25)

If your creditors learn you've lost your husband through widowhood, divorce, or separation, you stand a good chance of losing your credit, even though it's illegal to cancel it automatically.

Their views are archaic as well as illegal, but they're persistent. When the "breadwinner" goes, your credit can't be maintained, they think. Better to cancel first and ask questions later; otherwise, a creditor may find himself stuck with a large unpaid bill.

The law says that despite a change in your marital status, a creditor should make no changes in accounts for which you are contractually liable unless there's a strong reason to assume there's a problem. Only then can the creditor ask you questions. And only if the answers aren't satisfactory can a creditor cancel your credit. (26)

But widows constantly find their accounts closed when their husbands die and divorced women are asked to reapply for accounts they hold in good standing, though their husbands are not. A reapplication may be required only if the basis of the original account is your former spouse's income, but even then, the account must be left open while the creditor reevaluates you. (27)

If you were smart enough to establish credit in your own name while married, then you'll probably realize the only way a creditor will know you're not still married is if you tell him. Why send out divorce announcements? Just keep on using your good, separate credit. As long as you pay your bills on time you should have no problem.

To make the transition smoother, here's a piece of good news: creditors can't and usually won't ask whether you're divorced, widowed, or single. All they can legally ask is whether you are married, unmarried, or separated, that is if they are permitted to ask marital status at all. (See the law in Problem no. 16.)

Of course, if you do separate or divorce, you'll want to make sure your name is removed from any joint accounts. One woman told me she was miffed several years after her divorce to find her husband had given her now sixteen-year-old daughter her MasterCard. She had not removed her name from the account, so she would now be liable if her daughter ran up bills on it. That would make for worse than a family squabble—it could ruin her own credit if the bills went unpaid.

So far, we've focused on the plight of married and formerly married women. There's another kind of marital status discrimination—when people who are married are favored over people who aren't.

First, people who are married to each other are illegally favored as cosigners when the size of the transaction requires two signers. Any two qualified people have to be considered, whether renting an apartment or buying a home. If you've chosen a joint life-style alternative to marriage, remember the Equal Credit Opportunity Act covers you.

Second, if you are married and actually need a cosigner, a creditor might try to steer you toward your husband as that extra person. Resist if you want to establish credit. Bring another cosigner (a sister, aunt, parent, or friend), so there can't be any question later that it is your credit and not your spouse's. (28) Your friends and relatives might be a bit surprised at the request. Offer to return the favor someday. If you're really serious, offer to pay the debt through a third person, like an attorney, who can keep tabs and ensure you're not damaging your cosigner's credit with late payments.

There are a few exceptions to the marital status coverage of the Equal Credit Opportunity Act. Partial exemptions include securities transactions, utility credit, and business loans. In these, marital status provisions are altered or suspended, usually in the area of allowed inquiry. To be on firm ground, review Problem 25 in Table 3.

To wrap up, look at the Checklist for Married Women, page 90, and be sure you have covered your bases, if you are married. If not, you'll still want to do everything on the list.

Table 3. THE EQUAL CREDIT OPPORTUNITY ACT
AND REGULATION B—
MARITAL STATUS DISCRIMINATION

Problem 16

Creditors are often inclined to assume that in a marriage, the man controls the finances. For a woman it's best if separately qualified not to have to reveal your marital status. Then there can be no question as to who is in control.

Example: A woman living in Tennessee applies for credit and is asked by the bank officer if "her husband knows she's getting the loan?"

Solution: In this case, a separate property state, the inquiry, though informal, is illegal. It goes beyond marital status inquiry, which it is a backhand way of making, into an outrageous inquiry into whether the wife has the husband's permission to obtain the loan. Say so.

The Law: The language in the law itself left the door open to marital status inquiries in order to reflect differences in state laws.

"(b) It shall not constitute discrimination for purposes of this title for a creditor—

"(1) to make an inquiry of marital status if such inquiry is for the purpose of ascertaining the creditor's rights and remedies applicable to the particular extension of credit and not to discriminate in a determination of creditworthiness." [Sect. 701(b).]

Regulation B added:

"If an applicant applies for an individual, unsecured account, a creditor shall not request the applicant's marital status, unless the applicant resides in a community property state or property upon which the applicant is relying as a basis for repayment of the credit requested is located in such a state. Where an application is for other than individual, unsecured credit, a creditor may request an applicant's marital status. Only the terms 'married,' 'unmarried,' and 'separated' shall be used and a creditor may explain that the category 'unmarried' includes single, divorced, and widowed persons." [Regulation B, Sect. 202.5(d) (1).]

Problem 17

Married women are often asked to get their husbands to cosign loans even when this is not necessary.

Example: A middle-management executive in a midwestern city earning $25,000 a year is asked for her husband's cosignature for a MasterCard. She wants to get her card without involving her husband.

Solution: Tell the creditor that you expect her to follow the law and allow you to have the credit you are qualified for on your own. (Separate property state.)

The Law: Creditors are required to let a married (or unmarried) woman have credit without a cosigner if she meets the creditor's standards.

"A creditor shall not require the signature of an applicant's spouse or other person other than a joint applicant on any credit instrument if the applicant qualifies under the creditor's standards of creditworthiness for the amount in terms of the credit requested." [Regulation B, Sect. 202.7(d) (1).]

Problem 18

State laws vary, so Congress wanted to make sure that, where necessary, creditors could elicit spousal information.

Example: A Visa application in California requests that spousal information and cosignature be given. The housewife applying doesn't want to ask her husband to cosign.

Solution: The instances when information about your spouse can be requested are limited and information is not the same as cosigning, although creditors tend to confuse the two. It is legal in this instance to ask for the information, but not the cosignature. You'll need to cite the law, specifically including the section number, as this is one area of tremendous creditor resistance. You should know that some industry experts disagree with this author's interpretation. Some maintain that the only way for a creditor to eliminate the risk of each spouse independently committing the entire community property at different places at the same time is to require both signatures. Creditors and consumer representatives continue to disagree; as these legal issues are not settled, you might as well try to push for what is best for you.

The Law: "A creditor may request any information concerning an applicant's spouse . . . that may be requested about the applicant if:

"(i) the spouse will be permitted to use the account; or

"(ii) the spouse will be contractually liable upon the account; or

"(iii) the applicant is relying on the spouse's income as a basis for repayment of the credit requested; or

"(iv) the applicant resides in a community property state or property upon which the applicant is relying as a basis for repayment of the credit requested is located in such a state." [Regulation B, Sect. 202.5(c) (2).]

Problem 19
In community property states, married women are very frequently asked to get their husbands to cosign loans.

Example: A California housewife whose husband earns $65,000 per year wants to get a department store card but the woman in the credit office says she must take the application home for her husband to cosign.

Solution: If 50% of your community property will qualify you and you control it, you can commit these funds even though your husband "earns" them. If you don't know whether you control 50%, ask your state attorney general for a pamphlet on women's marital property rights.

The Law: See Problem 18.

Problem 20
Married women are often given joint credit even when they apply for credit alone.

Example: A woman is told "state law" prohibits giving her individual credit.

Solution: The Equal Credit Opportunity Act specifically allows state law to be preempted if you want separate credit, as long as you agree to be personally responsible.

The Law: "Any provision of State law which prohibits the separate extension of consumer credit to each party to a marriage shall not apply in any case where each party to a marriage voluntarily applies for separate credit from the same creditor: Provided, that in any case where such a State law is so preempted, each party to the marriage shall be solely responsible for the debt so contracted." [ECOA, Sect. 705(c).]

Problem 21

Often in real estate transactions, under the guise of getting a clear title, creditors will require a spouse to cosign a loan.

Example: An editor of a major metropolitan newspaper in California wants to purchase a piece of property in her own name. She's married and she earns enough to qualify without her husband's signature. The lender insists on his signing anyway.

Solution: Credit for property is one of the most complex areas. First, the fact that she, not he, earns the money is irrelevant as far as community property is concerned, since both their earnings are part of the community. Property is one area where both partners have to be involved, because it is assumed that the community acquires an interest in property acquired. The question is on what document can a creditor obtain both signatures in a secured transaction. In both community and separate property states a creditor may obtain a spouse's signature on the *security instrument* (the mortgage or deed of trust) as opposed to the bank note. This is so even if the spouses are not co-owners of the property. This is necessary in order to defeat the spouses' "spousal right" that is inchoate or existent by the terms of marital law until the time of death of one of the spouses. Accordingly, consumers should be aware that while a spouse can be required to sign the mortgage, he or she cannot be required to sign the note. For secured transactions not involving real property, such as a car, boat, or the like, an "integrated security statement," which combines the note and the security interest, is often illegal if it does not provide an opportunity for the nonapplicant to sign only the security interest and not the note.

The Law: The intention of the lawmakers was to enable a married woman, if she were creditworthy, to buy a home or property on her own, while protecting creditor rights, too.

"If an applicant requests secured credit, a creditor may require the signature of the applicant's spouse or other person on any instrument necessary, or reasonably believed by the creditor to be necessary, under applicable State law to make the property being offered as security available to satisfy the debt in the event of default, for example, any instrument to create a valid lien, pass clear title, waive inchoate rights, or assign earnings." [Regulation B, Sect. 202.7(d) (4).]

Problem 22
Married women's credit history is often nonexistent because credit is reported as the husband's.

Example: Mary Browning has a purseful of credit cards; some say "Mrs. Richard Browning"; some "Mrs. Mary Browning"; and some "Mr. and Mrs. Richard Browning." She applies for a Sears card and is turned down for insufficient credit references.

Solution: If you are a user on an account, you must make sure the account is reported in your name to the credit bureau or, for all practical purposes, you're nonexistent in the credit community. Make sure to obtain your credit report from the retail credit bureau, and advise the bureau and the reporting creditors how you want accounts reported.

The Law: Since 1977, all accounts that are opened must be reported in both spouses' names if both use the account.

"For every account established on or after June 1, 1977, a creditor that furnishes credit information shall:

"(i) determine whether an account offered by the creditor is one that an applicant's spouse is permitted to use or upon which the spouses are contractually liable other than as guarantors, sureties, endorsers, or similar parties; and

"(ii) designate any such account to reflect the fact or participation of both spouses." [Regulation B, Sect. 202.10(a) (1).]

Problem 23
If a man didn't pay his bills, a woman was stuck with his history, even if she herself had no control over his financial habits.

Example: Jerrie Jacobs married a financial slob, and now she's paying the price for his late payments. She needs an auto to get to work, but the auto company's bank won't finance her car, even though she's been divorced for two years and earns good money.

Solution: Tell the creditor the law recognizes your right to dissociate yourself from your spouse's bad history.

The Law: "A creditor shall consider, on the applicant's request, any information that the applicant may present tending to indicate that the credit history being considered by the creditor does not accurately reflect the applicant's creditworthiness." [Regulation B., Sect. 202.6(b) (6) (ii).]

Problem 24
Women's credit was automatically put under spouses' names even when they wanted to keep their professional or birth names.

Example: Jane Jones decided to keep her professional name when she married Harry Wyachsky, but several creditors notice she has designated Wyachsky as a user, and change her name anyway.

Solution: Tell the creditor the name you prefer and don't accept another.

The Law: "Designation of name. A creditor shall not prohibit an applicant from opening or maintaining an account in a birth-given first name and a surname that is the applicant's birth-given surname, the spouse's surname, or a combined surname." [Regulation B, Sect. 202.7(b).]

Problem 25
Married women and formerly married women need their spouses' credit histories to get credit, but the privacy laws made access difficult.

Example: A divorced woman wants to apply for credit, relying on her history of accounts shared for 20 years with her husband, but the creditor demands her husband give written permission before they will order his credit report.

Solution: Tell the creditor you have the right to use your former spouse's credit history without his signature.

The Law: "A creditor shall consider

"(i) the credit history, when available, of any account reported in the name of the applicant's spouse or former spouse that the applicant can demonstrate accurately reflects the applicant's creditworthiness." [Regulation B, sect. 202.6(b) (6) (i) and (iii).]

Problem 26

Creditors habitually cancel credit when notified of a change in marital status, usually because the woman changes her name or the husband cancels the credit at impending divorce.

Example: A divorced woman notifies creditors she's resuming her maiden or birth name, and creditors send her cancellation notices and application forms in reply.

Solution: Don't change your name. Get a credit identity and stick to it. But, in this instance, tell the creditor you are a contractually liable user and your card can't be terminated since you qualify for the card on your own.

The Law: "Action concerning existing open-end accounts. (1) In the absence of evidence of inability or unwillingness to repay, a creditor shall not take any of the following actions regarding an applicant who is contractually liable on an existing open-end account on the basis of the applicant's reaching a certain age or retiring, or on the basis of a change in the applicant's name or marital status:

"(i) require a reapplication; or

"(ii) change the terms of the account; or

"(iii) terminate the account." [Regulation B, Sect. 202.7(c) (1).]

Problem 27

A woman's credit rests solely on her husband's income, so she loses the credit at divorce.

Example: A professional woman still has her credit cards she got when she was in school and he earned the family living. Now she's getting a divorce and she's asked to reapply.

Solution: Tell the creditor you'll update their file to reflect your current income. A prevention tactic: If your earnings change substantially, let the creditor know before the need arises.

The Law: "A creditor may require a reapplication regarding an open-end account on the basis of a change in an applicant's marital status where the credit granted was based on income earned by the applicant's spouse if the applicant's income alone at the time of the original application would not support the amount of credit currently extended." [Regulation B, Sect. 202.7(c) (2).]

Problem 28
Married women who needed a cosigner were forced to use their husbands. Often this requirement would defeat their efforts to obtain separate credit.

Example: A married woman wants to buy a piece of lake property in Minnesota. The bank asks the married sister to have her husband cosign the loan even though her income is more than adequate. Because the buyer's income is too low to qualify on her own, she wants her employed sister to cosign, but the bank insists on the buyer's husband instead.

Solution: Tell the banker that a lender may not favor cosigners who are married to each other over other cosigners.

The Law: "The applicant's spouse may serve as an additional party, but a creditor shall not require that the spouse be the additional party." [Regulation B, Sect. 202.7(d) (5).]

CHECKLIST FOR MARRIED WOMEN

1. Have a bank account in your name.

2. Check your credit report.

3. Ask that all credit you use be reported in your given name and surname, "Lizzie Butler," not his, "Mrs. Bill Butler."

4. Obtain at least one bank card (MasterCard or Visa) in your own name, e.g. Lizzie Butler.

5. If you are not married now and plan to be, think carefully about leaving your credit in your own last name.

6. If you are married now, but your marriage is not secure, consider building a separate credit identity in your own "maiden" or birth name now. The law provides your right to credit in your maiden name if you so choose, and having credit of your own will make separation or divorce, if necessary, easier. (24)

5

Consumer Credit Protection Laws

In addition to the problems of women outlined in the preceding chapters, all consumers experience additional credit difficulties. Whether the problems are the result of an honest miscommunication or an unscrupulous creditor, consumers are protected by several laws. To be an aware credit consumer you should be aware of all the current legislation that provides avenues for resolution.

Just about now, you may be thinking you've signed up for a law course rather than bought a book! If you are a woman currently without credit, I suggest skipping this chapter and returning to it when you've gotten some. If, on the other hand, you've experienced difficulties with credit not related to sex or marital status, read on now!

CONSUMER CREDIT PROTECTION ACT

The first act passed in the late sixties to protect consumers was the Consumer Credit Protection Act, known as Truth in Lending. With its Regulation Z of the Federal Reserve System, the act has four major areas: disclosure, advertising, rescission, and liabilities.

Under disclosure, a creditor must tell you in writing how much the credit will cost you. This cost must be quoted in two ways—in the form of a finance charge and in the form of an annual percentage rate (APR). The finance charge is the total dollars and cents you will have to pay to borrow the money you need. The annual percentage rate is the relative cost of borrowing. It simply states the amount of interest and other finance charges per $100 borrowed per year. (29)

To ensure that creditors are honest in what they advertise, Truth in Lending has certain guidelines for advertising consumer credit. Creditors cannot advertise terms not regularly arranged with borrowers. The advertised rates must be those that are actually charged. Terms cannot be advertised unless they also specify the number, amount, and time span of payments.

This law also provides protection if you change your mind about certain credit situations. Under the rules of rescission, if you use your home as security for a loan, you have three business days after signing the agreement to cancel the contract. The rescission must be in writing and does not apply to the first mortgage on your home.

Under Truth in Lending, credit cards may only be issued upon request, rather than mailed out wholesale as in the past. Your liability as a card holder is limited to $50 in the case of unauthorized use. If you notify the issuer of the loss and theft before the card is used, then you are not liable for anything. (30)

CONSUMER LEASING ACT

The Consumer Leasing Act requires leasing companies to tell you the facts about the costs and terms of their contracts. The law applies to leases of personal property by an individual for a period of time more than four months and only for personal, family, or household use. It covers long-term rentals of cars, furniture, appliances, and other personal property. You can use the information to compare one lease with another or to compare the cost of leasing with the cost of buying. The law also limits any extra payment you may have to make at the end of a lease and regulates lease advertising.

Before you agree to a lease, the law requires that you get a written statement of all costs including any security deposit, license fees or taxes, and the total amount of your payments.

There is a distinction between open-end leases and closed-end leases. In a closed-end lease, you are not responsible for the value of the property upon return and therefore are paying a higher monthly payment than under open-end leases. In an open-end lease you run the risk of owing extra money depending on the value of the property when you return it. This special payment is termed a balloon payment. The Consumer Leasing Act limits a balloon payment to no more than three times the average monthly payment. There are also advertising regulations which apply to this act. Advertising must include the total of regular payments, your responsibilities at the end of the lease, and information about whether or not you may purchase the property. (31)

FAIR CREDIT REPORTING ACT

The Fair Credit Reporting Act covers operations of credit bureaus and other agencies that report and investigate consumers' credit ratings. (See chapter 7.) You are entitled to accurate and confidential credit reporting. An agency can give out information only to businesses with legitimate reasons for needing the information. This usually includes businesses to which you are applying for credit as well as prospective employers who want information on your past employment and income.

The act gives you specific rights if you are denied credit because of a credit bureau report. You are entitled to review your file with a member of the credit bureau's staff at no charge. If there are any mistakes, the bureau must investigate the items in question and make any necessary changes. Even if the item is not changed, you are entitled to file a one-hundred-word explanation. Your explanation must be included any time the bureau sends out the information in your file. (32)

As one Federal Trade Commission attorney pointed out, they receive more complaints about credit bureaus than any other credit area, so be persistent if you think you are right. But note, some bureaus will let you explain problems even if you were in the wrong, others will not. This area has not been settled definitively by the courts yet.

Congress passed the Fair Credit Billing Act to assist consumers in promptly correcting billing mistakes. The act applies only to open-end credit accounts, which include credit cards, revolving charge accounts, and overdraft checking.

If there is a mistake on your bill, you must notify the creditor in writing within sixty days after you receive the incorrect bill. The creditor must acknowledge your complaint within thirty days after your letter is received, unless the problem has already been resolved. Within two billing cycles, but not more than ninety days, the creditor must conduct an investigation and either correct the mistake or explain why the bill is correct. If the creditor did make a mistake, you will not have to pay finance charges on the disputed amount. However, if the creditor did not make an error, you will have to pay finance charges on the disputed amount and make up any missed payments.

FAIR CREDIT BILLING ACT

The Fair Credit Billing Act also provides that you can withhold payment on any damaged or defective goods or poor quality services purchased with a credit card. It is important that you first make an attempt to resolve the problem with the merchant. This right is limited if you use bank, travel, or entertainment cards rather than a card issued by a specific store. In such cases, your purchase must be for more than $50 and must have taken place in your home state or within 100 miles of your home address.

Pursuing a billing error remedy has more clout with creditors than the "damaged goods" complaint because the dispute resolution remedies are stronger. Here's an example. If you order a yellow carpet and you get a green one, this is not a dispute. It's a billing error, according to a Federal Trade Commission attorney who advises using a "billing error" rather than "dispute" method whenever possible.

Payments made to your account must be credited the same day they are received. The store is obligated to mail you a statement fourteen days before finance charges begin and provide you with a cash refund in case of an overpayment. (33)

FAIR DEBT COLLECTION PRACTICES ACT

The Fair Debt Collection Practices Act sets standards for the collection of any debt incurred for personal, family, or household purposes. A debt collector is defined as any person, other than the creditor or the creditor's attorney, who regularly col-

lects or attempts to collect debts owed to others. By this definition, only outside collectors the creditor may utilize and not
employees of the creditor are covered under the terms of
the act.

A debt collector may not contact you about your debt at an
unusual or inconvenient time or place, nor at work if your employer disapproves. If an attorney is representing you, all contact must be through your attorney.

You can stop a debt collector from contacting you by writing a letter to the collection agency telling them to stop. Once
they receive this letter, they may not contact you again except
to inform you of a specific action being taken.

Within five days after you are first contacted, the debt collector must send you a written notice telling you the amount of
money you owe; the name of the creditor to whom you owe the
money; and what to do if you feel you do not owe the money.

The debt collector may not contact you again if, within
thirty days after you are first contacted, you send the collector
a letter saying you do not owe the money, unless you are sent
proof of the debt.

In their collection practices, debt collectors are prohibited
from harassing, oppressing, or abusing consumers. They are
also prohibited from using any false statements in representing
themselves and the status of your debt. (34)

We'll see more about this in chapter 9.

THE BANKRUPTCY CODE

Bankruptcy is a viable solution to severe credit problems. The
decision to file should not be taken lightly. It should be thought
of as the final step after all other attempts to resolve your credit problems have failed.

The bankruptcy laws, which were revised and made more

consumer-oriented by the Bankruptcy Reform Act of 1978, establish an orderly and efficient procedure for relieving financially distressed debtors and, when appropriate, rehabilitates debtors without liquidating their assets.

There are two basic types of bankruptcy that are of concern to consumers: Chapter 7, known as "straight bankruptcy," and Chapter 13, known as the "wage earner's plan."

Under both plans, bankruptcy is initiated by filing a petition of bankruptcy with your local bankruptcy court. The court then orders an "order of relief" during which all creditors are prevented from contacting the debtor until the case is closed. The debtor must, at this time, submit a list of all creditors, a schedule of all assets and liabilities, and surrender to a trustee all property and recorded information relating to the property. Under Chapter 7, the trustee takes title to all property and makes an equitable distribution. No preferences can be given to a particular creditor. Chapter 7 allows certain property to be exempted from this proceeding. These exemptions are usually items "necessary for ordinary life in modern society," "necessary for the support of the debtor and dependents," and "property up to $7,500 in value." It must be understood that under Chapter 7, the debtor is released only from the liabilities listed; debts not listed may still be owed. Also, some debts cannot be discharged, including student loans and fraudulently acquired debts. Once a debtor has discharged all debts through Chapter 7, bankruptcy cannot be filed again for another seven years.

Chapter 13 is a milder form of filing bankruptcy. A fifth of all personal filings are under this form and the numbers are rising. It is a vehicle for the rehabilitation of the debtor without liquidation of assets. Chapter 13 can either extend the allotted time for repayment or reduce the debt by requiring less than full repayment of debts.

Not all debtors can file under Chapter 13. You must have a

regular income and owe less than $100,000 in liquid unsecured debts. The plan prescribes the amount that the debtor must surrender to a trustee every payday. The amount is usually calculated by subtracting monthly expenses from monthly income. For the program to be set up, the debtor must take home more than is required in the household budget. A Chapter 13 plan will not last longer than three years, although special conditions can extend it to five years. Chapter 13 helps to preserve your credit rating and has no time limit between filings.

You also should be aware that many state laws allow you to keep more property, so in many cases following state law is preferable. This is just one of several reasons you should work through an attorney if you find yourself in this critical situation.

ELECTRONIC FUND TRANSFER ACT

Electronic banking has grown tremendously over the past few years. New technology has produced automatic teller machines, point of sale terminals, preauthorized transfers, and telephone transfers. To keep up with consumer protection in this new area, Congress passed the Electronic Fund Transfer Act.

The act requires that your periodic bank statement show all electronic transfers to and from your account, including those made at electronic terminals, by a preauthorized arrangement, or under a telephone transfer plan. Your monthly statement is proof of payment to another person, your record for tax or other purposes, and your way of checking and reconciling electronic fund transfer (EFT) transactions with your bank balance.

If you believe that there has been an error in your electronic fund transfer, you must write or call your financial institution no later than sixty days from the time the first statement with the error was mailed. The financial institution must promptly investigate an error and resolve it within forty-five days. If the financial institution takes longer than ten business days to complete the investigation, it must recredit your account for the amount in question while it finishes the investigation. You must be notified concerning the results of its investigation and the financial institution must supply you with copies of investigation documents if you request them.

The consumer's liability for an unauthorized withdrawal is limited to $50 only if the financial institution is notified within two business days after you have learned of the loss or theft of your card. You can lose as much as $500 if you do not report the loss or theft within the two days. If you do not report an unauthorized transfer that appears on your statement within sixty days, you risk unlimited loss. (35)

Congress passed consumer protection legislation for your benefit. Now you know your rights: take advantage of them. You can use the law directly by asserting your rights to the creditor. If direct action fails, call on others to intervene for you. A lawyer can always be brought in—if only to write a letter on your behalf—and you can also use the enforcing agencies. Although many of them do not process individual complaints, a letter to the agency will often spur the creditor into action. I suggest sending a carbon copy to the appropriate agency when you are confronting a creditor with a problem along these lines, since for many of those agencies their law enforcement investigation targets are the result of unsolicited consumer complaints.

Please see Appendix 2 for a list of agencies to write to for assistance. You'll find the address of the Women's Credit and Finance Project in Appendix 3.

Remember, consumer laws only operate if consumers

know how to challenge traditional business practices that violate these laws. Use the law to fight back.

Table 4. CONSUMER CREDIT PROTECTION ACT
TRUTH IN LENDING
CONSUMER LEASING ACT
FAIR CREDIT REPORTING ACT
FAIR CREDIT BILLING ACT
FAIR DEBT COLLECTION PRACTICES ACT
ELECTRONIC FUND TRANSFER ACT

Problem 29

Consumers often thought they were paying one rate when it turned out the interest rate was much higher.

Example: Dorothy Starr goes to get a car loan and is told that the interest rate is $8\frac{1}{2}\%$. She's not the kind of person who reads the fine print, and when she gets home she discovers that the interest rate is actually $8\frac{1}{2}\%$ for one year and then it jumps to 10% and then to 12%.

Solution: Look at any credit contract carefully. By law today it has to show the APR (Annual Percentage Rate), which takes into account all of the various parts of interest charged on any given loan and comes up with one simple rate that is an expression of the whole.

The Law: Consumer Credit Protection Act, Sect. 106, 107.

Problem 30

Credit card theft and fraud is growing. Sometimes consumers' cards are stolen. In other cases the numbers are stolen and thousands of dollars charged by phone.

Example: Frances May receives her Diners Club bill and finds that she has been charged for several thousand dollars in travel tickets that are not hers. She is extremely upset. In addition to notifying Diners Club, she calls her insurance agent to inquire about credit fraud insurance.

Solution: Under Truth in Lending, your liability is limited to $50 if your card is used without your authority and if the use occurs before you notify the creditor.

The Law: Consumer Credit Protection Act, Sect. 133.

Problem 31

Many consumers are now leasing cars and other items and questions arise about the true costs of these items.

Example: Ms. Jones decides to lease a car rather than buy one. When she tries to compare the costs of leasing to current bank automobile lending rates, she finds that the lease, which appeared cheaper, is actually almost 40% more expensive.

Solution: Make sure seller provides you with a full statement of costs and conditions of any lease.

The Law: Consumer Credit Protection Act, Title V, Consumer Leasing Act, Sect. 181–186.

Problem 32

Consumers have lost credit and jobs because of contents of credit reports. These contents were held secret and often, even if they were inaccurate, they were difficult to change.

Example: John Dinkman is turned down for several high security jobs. Finally, one prospective employer tells him, "Your credit performance has us worried."

Solution: See your credit report before you look for a job or get credit. Often, mistakes creep in. Correct any errors, and if you have had problems, tell the potential creditor before he sees the bad news.

The Law: Consumer Credit Protection Act, Title VI, Fair Credit Reporting Act, Sect. 601–622.

Problem 33

Consumers continue to be billed for mistakes or for items that don't work.

Example: Jewel Van Marble buys a new washing machine from the May Company and after it is installed the machine won't work. She returns the washer, but is billed for it for several months. Jewel decides to write the Credit Department and tells them she is being billed for an item that was returned, but all she gets in reply is a form letter. Several months later Jewel applies for credit elsewhere and is turned down because of late payment on her May Company account.

Solution: The store has failed to honor the terms of the Fair Credit Billing Act. Once the situation reaches this stage, your credit rating is affected. If you cannot get an answer, you may want to consider paying the money in escrow to an attorney who will in turn notify the store that he or she is holding the money pending resolution of the problem.

This is also a good time to put your 100-word consumer explanation into the credit file.

The Law: Consumer Credit Protection Act, Fair Credit Billing Act, Sect. 161–171.

Problem 34

Consumers are often harassed by unscrupulous collectors.

Example: Jeanie Farnsworth is behind on her payments to the ABC Oil Company. In the last week, she has received three rude calls at her job about the debt.

Solution: You cannot be called at your place of work if it violates your employer's rules. Furthermore, it is illegal for a collector to harass you. Three calls in a week qualifies as harassment. The law also says you can't be spoken to in abusive language. Tell all of this to the debt collector, and tell him not to contact you anymore.

The Law: Consumer Credit Protection Act, Title VII, Fair Debt Collection Practices Act, Sect. 801–818.

Problem 35

Electronic funds transfer may result in large errors or thefts directly from a consumer account.

Example: Mrs. Smallwood's purse is stolen in a shopping center. In the purse is the ATM (Automatic Teller Machine) card and her PIN (Personal Identification Number) is written where the thief discovers it. The thief withdraws $750 from Mrs. Smallwood's account. Can she get this money back?

Solution: The Electronic Fund Transfer Act provides protection for you if you report the loss within 60 days of the time the bank mails out a statement reflecting such a loss and you report the loss within two days after you learn of it. If it takes you longer to report the loss, you can be charged up to $500.

The Law: Consumer Credit Protection Act, Title IX, Electronic Fund Transfer Act, Sect. 901–921.

Part Three

GETTING CREDIT

6

The Credit You Want

If you don't have credit, by now you're probably convinced you ought to. But where do you start?

To build your credit you must be systematic. We've all heard the old saw that you should open a savings account, then take out a loan against that, pay it off, and *voilà*, your credit is established. But the system has changed dramatically in the last few years.

My method, developed for today's financial scene, is different. All the savings/collateral method will give you is one positive entry on your credit report—a limited base from which to build an entire credit portfolio.

Instead, go for the credit wonder tool, the bank card, more popularly known as Visa or MasterCard. With a bank card, you have an entrée into credit from better department stores, for many of them will open an account on the spot if you already have a Visa or MasterCard. With a few department store cards in hand, and a period of active, conscientious use, you're ready for a travel card, auto loan, or, if resources permit, a mortgage.

Perhaps you've already tried for a bank card and been turned down. Chances are, you went about it wrong. Probably, you saw a form at the bank or even in a restaurant, filled it in, and sent if off to a centralized processing center. If you didn't already have other credit, you'd most likely be turned down for "no credit file" or "insufficient credit file." You do have to have credit to get it, but there are a couple of ways around this Catch-22.

The first and best way is to get the support of your banker, who can actually initial your bank card application, thereby indicating his/her preliminary approval. Then the remote processing center had better have a good reason if they turn you down.

You're probably thinking, "That's fine for people who have a banker. I just have a checking account and I bank by mail, so I don't even know the tellers." Unless you keep your money under the mattress, you do have a banker. But if you're like many women, you may not know your bank president or bank manager.

At a meeting of successful women in the film industry, I asked how many women in the audience had taken their banker to lunch. One hand came up.

Yet as my bank president, Linda Fluent, points out, "A good banker will always take time to meet with you." And Sarah Kovner, chair of the First Women's Bank of New York, concurs: "Certainly I'm available to our customers. That's part of my job as head of the bank." The bank president doesn't want to have you call about routine matters, but a savvy customer knows and is known by the head person in the bank, if it's a small one, or the branch manager in a larger institution.

So what are you waiting for? Get an appointment to meet your banker today!

When you meet, take a filled-in application so you won't

have to hem and haw, searching for answers. Find out exactly what the criteria are for a bank card at your bank. If you meet them, ask your banker to initial your application, and you should be on your way to establishing credit. If you don't qualify, let the banker know that you intend to return and that you'd like to count on her support then. In the meanwhile, pursue the second kind of bank card, a debit card.

A debit card looks exactly like a credit card, but rather than billing you later (credit), the card draws (debits) against a cash balance. The only drawbacks are that you have to be able to locate an institution that offers them and you have to have the necessary cash.

Almost all the "cash management accounts" (CMA's) or money market accounts at stock brokerage houses offer debit cards, some debit MasterCards and Visas, and a few, an American Express Gold debit card. These accounts are great for people with plenty of cash, because you have the convenience of instant plastic access to your cash. But if you're not well heeled enough to open a $20,000 to $25,000 account, what then? Fortunately, there are also some banks and savings and loans around the country that do offer debit cards, even if you have as little as $300 in an account. Ask your banker for a debit card. If your bank doesn't offer one, then ask him to help you find one. (See Appendix 3.)

Now with either the credit or debit card in hand, you're ready for the next step. Two or three good department stores should join your list of creditors next. You can help them do so by presenting yourself, usually right on the sales floor, with Visa, MasterCard, American Express, or Diners Club in hand. With this card in your name, most better department stores will establish an account for you instantly.

Here's how it works. They use your bank card as a reference, establish a small account to cover your current purchase, check out your credit record, and if there's nothing amiss, send you a card. Since you don't have credit, except for the bank card, you certainly won't be disqualified by a negative item on your credit.

Now you're on your way. As you add to your credit, don't apply for too many accounts at once. Creditors get alarmed when they see a string of "inquiries" on your credit report, suggesting the possibility that you're on a spending spree.

FIVE STEPS TO ESTABLISH CREDIT

1. Establish a relationship with your bank or savings and loan company.

2. Meet the president or manager.

3. Apply for Visa/MasterCard.

4. Get department store cards using your bank card as reference.

5. Check with your credit bureau to be sure your accounts are being reported.

This method, as summarized above, sounds so easy, you'd wonder why anyone would ever have trouble getting credit. But our hotline calls show that they do. Let's look at a few problem cases and solutions so you'll be equipped to handle the unexpected.

The first snag is that people don't follow the method exactly. It doesn't work if you cut corners. Perhaps you're a bit shy and you think, "I'll just go in and if the manager's busy, see the assistant manager." Of course the manager will be busy if you don't call ahead for an appointment. So you end up being sidetracked to someone below the top. Or, you decide to stop by on the way back from the market, with the car full of children, dogs, and groceries; you feel harried and you show it. Take yourself seriously and plan ahead before you tackle any credit situation.

But, it's not always the woman's fault—many times the system doesn't take us seriously. Although no one who has tried the Five Steps method has reported failure, many women who've applied other ways have faced rejection. Sometimes, it's a clear-cut case of illegal behavior on the part of the creditor, but often a marginally qualified woman is turned down where a similarly qualified man would not be.

All too frequently, women calling our hotline report that their applications are not answered within the thirty-day limit, they're not given reasons for rejection, creditors have turned them down for incomplete or incorrect information on their credit report, or they encounter creditors who still won't honor the law and give separate credit to married women, as one Los Angeles woman learned.

Mrs. Browning has tried repeatedly to get credit in her own name. She has several joint accounts with her husband, but each time she applies for an account in her own name, she's turned down. One creditor says they cannot issue separate accounts to someone who already has a joint account, another wants her husband to cosign, and another cites her lack of credit history.

As we've seen in the last chapter, on all these counts, Mrs. Browning has the law on her side, but she must make sure creditors apply it. If you are married, don't put yourself in the position of battering your head against a brick wall. Before you go out to apply, get your joint and user credit reported in your name and review the law (table 3 in chapter 4).

With your joint and user credit now reported, here's a

shortcut on the Five Steps method. If you're married, make sure your joint accounts have your own name on your card. You can do this by simply asking, since the law requires that creditors honor this request. Now, with a Visa, MasterCard, American Express, or Diners Club plastic with your own name on it, you can go to department stores and get a few accounts of your own. After using them and paying your bills on time, you're established separately. The next stop is back to your bank for a Visa or MasterCard of your very own. This method may not work if you're a nonearning homemaker in a separate property state, although some department stores will still give you an account based on your husband's earnings and your privilege, as a wife, to have "necessaries," an old common law term for personal needs. Otherwise, your best bet would be to make sure that as many accounts as possible are in both your names and that they're reported as such.

Perhaps the situation isn't clear-cut.

Ms. Henning from Bell Gardens, with an $11,000 income and $75,000 in liquid assets, was denied a MasterCard, but then she received a Visa with a $500 limit from a different bank. Next she applied for an American Express card, but was turned down for insufficient income. She'd like to extend her credit limit on her Visa, but with the negative results with American Express, she's not sure what credit line to expect.

Ms. Henning's case illustrates several key points. First, there are definite stages of credit life. A middle-aged woman earning $11,000 a year will be denied an American Express card. By contrast a student just graduating from college with promised earnings of $10,000 will be actively solicited, complete with preppie posters, by the same company. Why? Because the assumption is that the student's position in life will steadily improve, while the middle-aged woman has peaked out. But what about the woman who has recently returned to the work force? Her earnings may rise quickly too, once she's established. Presently, the credit system doesn't take women's special life patterns into account, as discussed in chapter 1. If you don't enter the credit system at the appointed time and remain active, you can expect to be penalized for being out of tune with your age-set.

Second, Ms. Henning's case illustrates a key credit problem for all consumers: Creditors don't ordinarily reveal their credit criteria, so how can a consumer judge her chances in the credit arena?

The credit you get will depend on general standards and the specific criteria of your potential creditors.

Bankers and other creditors use the "three C's" as a shorthand way of referring to the general rules for evaluating potential customers, so you should know and understand them. They are: Character, Capacity, and Collateral.

Creditors believe that people with character—integrity and fortitude—will pay their bills even in the face of difficulties. No legal safeguards will protect the creditor if character is lacking, since our system allows "welshing on a commitment," to quote a banker's manual.

Bankers believe that character is an inner quality and not something immediately visible. Some people claim to size up a person after a brief face-to-face encounter, but smart bankers know that character is not easily read. According to current thinking, an astute credit grantor looks at reputation and background.

How are these ephemerals such as "reputation" and "background" judged? Popular standards include "length of residence" and "length of time employed." The assumption is that people who stay put on their job and at their home will be better risks than people who are mobile. That's why you'll find boxes on applications asking your residence for the past five years. Most creditors have established minimum residence and job requirements, and for bank cards, a minimum of time with an account at that institution. These criteria reflect attitudes of yesteryear, but they're all used as character indicators today.

In our mobile society, these outmoded concepts would disqualify too many perfectly profitable customers, so for most consumer credit, your credit record serves as a reference, which is one reason it's so important. Being known to your banker would be especially important for the same reason.

With the weight assigned to individual personality or character, you can see why women have trouble. Both our personalities and expectations about them are different.

The second of the three C's is capacity, or your ability to pay. If you don't earn enough, if what you earn is already committed elsewhere, or if you haven't earned it long enough to assure the creditor it's reliable, then you fail the capacity test.

Most creditors set minimum earnings standards. The best way to find out is to ask in each situation. Creditors are in the habit of not having to explain because not many people do ask. Most will give you some sense of their standards. For example, Visa and MasterCard are set on a bank-by-bank basis, but usually an income of $750 a month is minimum. In 1983, American Express required $15,000 per year for the green card and $20,000 for the gold. But, Meredith Fernstrom, senior vice-president, reminds us, "Don't just look at income and assume that's all it takes. American Express looks at a combination of factors on our credit scoring system. The minimum income is not sufficient if it's not stable, the level of debt is too high, or a person has an unfavorable credit report or no report at all."

Creditors look at existing debt to see if you are overcom-

114

mitted. As a rule of thumb, the creditor would like no more than 18 to 20 percent of your current income to go toward fixed obligations, excluding mortgage or rent. For home purchases, lenders would like your mortgage to be no more than 25 percent of your gross monthly income. (See Table 5.) I've dubbed this formula the "45 percent rule of thumb:" housing 25 percent + other debts 20 percent = 45 percent maximum monthly debt.

There are instances for which creditors will make exceptions, particularly in mortgage credit where a "highly motivated" buyer may be willing to sacrifice many other purchases in order to be a homeowner. Lenders will sometimes allow that special person to commit up to 40 percent of income for housing, provided that there are no other substantial consumer debts. (To keep all this in perspective, according to the government's annual housing survey, the poor spend 72 percent of their earnings on rental housing.)

Table 5. LENDER'S RULE OF THUMB FOR MORTGAGES

Annual Income

2 to 2.5 times annual income = House price

Example: • Your annual take-home pay is $24,000
• You can afford a house in the $48–60,000 price range (2 to $2\frac{1}{2}$ × 24,000 = 48–60,000)

Monthly Income

Monthly mortgage × 4 = Total monthly gross income

Example: $1,000/month mortgage × 4 = $4,000 per month gross income needed to qualify.

With these rules of thumb, look at the impact of rising interest rates on qualifying for a mortgage. Let's see what happens when the interest rises on a $100,000 mortgage for 30 years. At 10 percent the interest is $877 per month; at 12 percent, $1,028 per month; and at 15 percent, $1,264 per month. The five-point spread in interest rates makes a $387-a-month difference. A jump of a single point can disqualify you for a loan. If you needed $3,388 per month income to qualify at 10 percent and the interest rate jumped 2 points to 12 percent, then you'd need $4,012 income a month to qualify for the exact same home. That's over $600 a month difference in income. From this example, you can see that being qualified, even in the income setting, depends upon a set of shifting parameters that the market, as well as your own income, can affect.

As a measure of your own income reliability, the presumption is that the longer you've earned a certain amount, the more likely you are to continue to do so. That's where phrases such as "she's a fifty-thousand-dollar-a-year woman" originate. You take on your earning capacity like a cloak.

Creditors don't trust unearned income. Whether from investment earnings, pensions, annuities, or alimony, the objection to derivative income is it doesn't rest upon your current personal efforts. So in Ms. Henning's case, the fact that she has $75,000 in liquid assets is less telling than the size of her $11,000 income.

If character reflects your willingness to pay and capacity reflects your ability, then collateral tells how you'll pay if character or capacity fail. If Ms. Henning had been applying for a collateralized loan, her $75,000 assets would have made a difference, for collateral is what she would lose if she didn't honor her promise to pay.

If you get overextended on your bills or lose your job,

creditors expect you'll draw on your savings, stocks, or property to honor the obligation. That's one reason you should exercise special care not to overextend yourself on mortgage credit—the unexpected expenses of homeownership combined with too small an income-to-debt ratio can lead to loss of your property and your original investment. For the average middle-income consumer today, a credit rating often replaces collateral, since it will reflect how available you made what money you did have.

The three C system sounds simple enough. Why would Ms. Henning or anyone else have trouble with it?

Answer: Because it's as subjective as can be! How could a banker seriously claim to evaluate your willingness to pay (character) on your personal style (see how important it is to dress for success?). The assumption that the well-dressed person is more trustworthy flies in the face of egalitarianism, yet that's exactly how the system works.

In order to get rid of this kind of irrational judgment, well-meaning creditors (who not coincidentally also had to process mountains of applications) devised a method called the "credit score" for sorting people out numerically.

Your credit score, like your credit rating, is a construct that changes according to who's keeping the scoreboard. Typically, the credit score is simply a system of assigning numerical values to your particular characteristics as a credit applicant. The factors used are generally similar, although there's no standard "credit score." A sample is given in Table 6 on page 118.

Credit scoring also has its drawbacks. Most scoring systems were developed before many women had credit, so the universe they measure does not fully include women's experience. A person who is a "professional" is given 27 points on the sample, but service workers, like waitresses, only get 14

Table 6. CREDIT SCORING

Characteristics

Home phone .... +36
Own your residence .... +34
Have other finance company (are you in debt?) .... −12
Have bank credit card .... +29
Checking or savings account .... +13
Checking and savings account .... +19

Occupation

Professionals and officials .... +27
Technicians and managers .... + 5
Proprietors .... − 3
Clerical and sales .... +12
Craftsmen and non-farm laborers 0
Foremen and operators .... +26
Service workers .... +14
Farmworkers .... + 3

Age

30 or under .... + 6
Over 30 to 40 .... +11
Over 40 to 50 .... + 8
Over 50 .... +16

Years on Job

Less than 5 0
More than 5 and up to 15 .... + 6
More than 15 .... +18

points. Yet until very recently, few women entered professions, so a well-paid waitress was penalized twice, first excluded from a high-earning career, then from the credit system
because of job choice.

Let's look at how the credit scoring system worked for one
consumer, Ms. Strong, who forwarded a rejection letter from a
creditor, which said in part:

> We have reviewed your application which we are unable to
> approve.
>
> We use a credit scoring system in reviewing applications
> for charge cards. This system works by giving points to
> certain credit characteristics which we obtained from your
> application. The number of points you get depends on a sta-
> tistical analysis of how closely your credit characteristics
> compare to those of applicants with whom we have had
> good experience. You did not receive enough points to
> qualify for the credit requested. The characteristics we
> scored which most significantly contributed to our decision
> are listed below in ascending order, beginning with the fac-
> tor which requires the least amount of change.
>
> > Excessive financial obligations
> > Our experience with your occupational group
> > Our experience with non-homeowners
>
> Credit scoring is a complex area and you should under-
> stand that no single credit characteristic causes the issu-
> ance or denial of credit. If you are able to change one or
> more of the above characteristics, you may come closer to
> our statistical model, but still may not receive enough
> points.

A letter like this points out the frustrations consumers
have with the system, for as it indicates, Ms. Strong could im-

prove her position on any factor and still fail on other counts. A person who has failed to obtain an adequate score on a credit scoring system and who has a subjectively excellent history, should make her or his case known to decision-makers in the company and request an "override" because of an "anomaly" in the system. Remember, all we're talking about here is whether Ms. Strong will pay her bill, but credit scoring systems tend to take on a life of their own, transcending and transgressing the original purposes for which they were created.

That's why I say let's modify credit scoring systems along "comparable worth" lines and make credit criteria known. What's wrong with sending a letter that states in plain, straightforward English:

> We couldn't approve your credit request. In order to qualify, you would need an income of $15,000 per year and your other debts shouldn't exceed $150 per month. When you meet these standards, please reapply.

Creditors say: This opens the way to cheating! If people knew our criteria, they would stretch the truth to fit. There are criminals who make their living from creating fraudulent applications. These criminals already know enough about the system to manipulate it anyway. Even so, losses from fraudulent applications were reported at only $8 million in 1983 contrasted to the $66 billion in credit card transactions in the same year. The entire credit system rests on people's honesty. If consumers cheated in large numbers, the system would fall apart now. If more honest people know how things work, then the system will benefit, because fraud often involves duping honest people or encroaching on their credit records by interlopers.

With all this effort going into credit judgments, it's obvious that filling out your credit application properly is vital.

The credit application is a short financial statement. It should be written in accordance with accounting principles, the language of business. One of the first things that you learn when you take a class in accounting at the Harvard Business School is that accounting is not the rigid "there-is-only-one-right-answer" system that you might have been led to believe all your life. Like a language, "some of its rules are definite, whereas others are not." Accounting is subject to interpretation.

Your accounting truths (financial statement) and credit truths (loan form) must mesh to paint you favorably and at the same time portray you honestly.

I've found women don't know how to present themselves properly in two key areas, "gross" versus "net" income and "book" versus "market" value.

For salary, always list your gross or before-tax salary, unless a form specifies net or after-tax salary. Most lenders' rules of thumb are based on gross salary, but many uninformed consumers list their take-home pay, thus undermining their chances.

Likewise, if you're estimating your assets, make sure to list the "market value" or current sales price rather than "book value" or price paid originally. Especially for real estate, antiques, foreign cars, precious metals, stones, and collectibles, you may be pleasantly surprised at their—and your—worth.

On the obligation side of the balance sheet, always show outstanding obligations by their current face amount. If a mortgage has been paid down, reflect that on your statement. Or, if you have a loan, list only the principal due, since technically you don't owe the interest until it becomes due.

Don't ever offer any negative information about yourself and don't volunteer information not requested. For example, don't state that you're divorced, just put "unmarried" if the marital status box requires your reply.

[Open end, unsecured credit]

CREDIT APPLICATION

IMPORTANT: Read these Directions before completing this Application.

Check
Appropriate
Box

☐ If you are applying for an individual account in your own name and are relying on your own income or assets and not the income or assets of another person as the basis for repayment of the credit requested, complete only Sections A and D.

☐ If you are applying for a joint account or an account that you and another person will use, complete all Sections, providing information in B about the joint applicant or user.

☐ If you are applying for an individual account, but are relying on income from alimony, child support, or separate maintenance or on the income or assets of another person as the basis for repayment of the credit requested, complete all Sections to the extent possible, providing information in B about the person on whose alimony, support, or maintenance payments or income or assets you are relying.

SECTION A—INFORMATION REGARDING APPLICANT

Full Name (Last, First, Middle): .... Birthdate: / /

Present Street Address: .... Years there: ....

City: .... State: .... Zip: .... Telephone: ....

Social Security No.: .... Driver's License No.: ....

Previous Street Address: .... Years there: ....

City: .... State: .... Zip: ....

Present Employer: .... Years there: .... Telephone: ....

Position or title: .... Name of supervisor: ....

Employer's Address: ....

Previous Employer: .... Years there: ....

Previous Employer's Address: ....

Present net salary or commission: $ .... per .... No. Dependents: .... Ages: ....

Alimony, child support, or separate maintenance income need not be revealed if you do not wish to have it considered as a basis for repaying this obligation.

Alimony, child support, separate maintenance received under: court order ☐ written agreement ☐ oral understanding ☐

Other income: $ .... per .... Source(s) of other income: ....

Is any income listed in this Section likely to be reduced in the next two years?
☐ Yes (Explain in detail on a separate sheet.) No ☐

Have you ever received credit from us? .... When? .... Office: ....

Checking Account No.: .... Institution and Branch: ....

Savings Account No.: .... Institution and Branch: ....

Name of nearest relative
not living with you: .... Telephone: ....

Relationship: .... Address: ....

SECTION B—INFORMATION REGARDING JOINT APPLICANT, USER, OR OTHER PARTY (Use separate sheets if necessary.)

Full Name (Last, First, Middle): .... Birthdate: / /

Relationship to Applicant (if any): ....

Present Street Address: .... Years there: ....

City: .... State: .... Zip: .... Telephone: ....

Social Security No.: .... Driver's License No.: ....

Present Employer: .... Years there: .... Telephone: ....

Position or title: .... Name of supervisor: ....

Employer's Address: ....

Previous Employer: .... Years there: ....

Previous Employer's Address: ....

Present net salary or commission: $ .... per .... No. Dependents: .... Ages: ....

Alimony, child support, or separate maintenance income need not be revealed if you do not wish to have it considered as a basis for repaying this obligation.

Alimony, child support, separate maintenance received under: court order ☐ written agreement ☐ oral understanding ☐

Other income: $ .... per .... Source(s) of other income: ....

Is any income listed in this Section likely to be reduced in the next two years?
☐ Yes (Explain in detail on a separate sheet.) ☐ No

Checking Account No.: .... Institution and Branch: ....

Savings Account No.: .... Institution and Branch: ....

Name of nearest relative not living
with Joint Applicant, User, or Other Party: .... Telephone: ....

Relationship: .... Address: ....

SECTION C—MARITAL STATUS
(Do not complete if this is an application for an individual account.)

Applicant: ☐ Married ☐ Separated ☐ Unmarried (including single, divorced, and widowed)

Other Party: ☐ Married ☐ Separated ☐ Unmarried (including single, divorced, and widowed)

SECTION D—ASSET AND DEBT INFORMATION (If Section B has been completed, this Section should be completed giving information about both the Applicant and Joint Applicant, User, or Other Person. Please mark Applicant-related information with an "A." If Section B was not completed, only give information about the Applicant in this Section.)

ASSETS OWNED (Use separate sheet if necessary.)

Description of Assets	Value	Subject to Debt? Yes/No	Name(s) of Owner(s)
Cash	$		
Automobiles (Make, Model, Year)			
Cash Value of Life Insurance (Issuer, Face Value)			
Real Estate (Location, Date Acquired)			
Marketable Securities (Issuer, Type, No. of Shares)			
Other (List)			
Total Assets	$		

OUTSTANDING DEBTS (Include charge accounts, instalment contracts, credit cards, rent, mortgages, etc. Use separate sheet if necessary.)

Creditor	Type of Debt or Acct. No.	Name in Which Acct. Carried	Original Debt	Present Balance	Monthly Payments	Past Due? Yes/No
1. (Landlord or Mortgage Holder)	☐ Rent Payment ☐ Mortgage		$ (Omit rent)	$ (Omit rent)	$	
2.						
3.						
4.						
5.						
6.						
Total Debts			$	$	$	

(Credit References)   Date Paid

1. $

2.

Are you a co-maker, endorser, or guarantor on any loan or contract?   Yes ☐   No ☐   If "yes" for whom?   To whom?

Are there any unsatisfied judgments against you?   Yes ☐   No ☐   Amount $ If "yes" to whom owed?

Have you been declared bankrupt in the last 14 years?   Yes ☐   No ☐   If "yes" where?   Year

Other Obligations—(E.g., liability to pay alimony, child support, separate maintenance. Use separate sheet if necessary.)

Everything that I have stated in this application is correct to the best of my knowledge. I understand that you will retain this application whether or not it is approved. You are authorized to check my credit and employment history and to answer questions about your credit experience with me.

_____   _____   _____   _____
Applicant's Signature   Date   Other Signature (Where Applicable)   Date

To avoid last-minute scrambling for account numbers, keep a complete sample application in your file. Use the one on pages 122–123 as a model, or pick one up at any bank. Be sure to review your credit report and don't omit any accounts shown in the report, since creditors look for consistency between the two. Each time you apply for credit, be sure to keep a copy of your application. All too frequently consumers don't receive a response, and without a copy they have no proof of having applied.

Now let's turn from lender criteria to your own. Many readers of this book will be more than qualified for credit. With a range of choices, how do you know what kind of credit to get?

Often consumers are confused by all the names given to different credit accounts. I've developed the "six basics of credit" to simplify your thinking. These six basics will allow you to cut through the jargon and see the essentials clearly.

1. Who—keeps your credit report and who's reported on it.
2. What—is the amount of credit, payment, interest, and prepayment penalty.
3. When—you have to pay.
4. Where—you can use the credit (stores, banks, filling stations, restaurants).
5. Why—you have to pay (what you will lose if you don't, your credit standing or collateral).
6. How—to get credit.

In most instances, it makes less difference than people imagine whether you have an installment loan or a revolving charge account or a bank card or a credit union account. The exceptions are if the account is due in thirty days or if you have a prepayment penalty for early retirement of the loan. It may also make a difference for credit history purposes. And, having a mortgage or leveraged investment, for which you need credit, can make a big difference. So that you will feel confident if someone starts throwing around credit jargon, Table 7 reviews credit definitions and Table 8 summarizes kinds of credit.

Table 7. CREDIT DEFINITIONS

1. **Noninstallment**   Noninstallment credit includes open-ended credit cards, single payment loans due in 30, 60, or 90 days, and "service credit," debts to doctors, hospitals, utilities, and other establishments that serve you.

2. **Installment**   Credit scheduled for two or more payments, including revolving credit.

3. **Unsecured**   Unsecured credit is credit on which you have pledged an income stream.

4. **Secured**   A specific asset is pledged. If you default, you must forfeit the asset.

Table 8. HOW MAJOR CREDIT WORKS

1. **Open-ended**   Charge up to your limit every month, pay it off every 30 days. Usually no interest if paid on time. Example, department stores.

2. **Revolving**   Overall limit is lower and usually you have a set amount to pay each month.

3. **Bank cards**   Limits generally between $300 and $3,000. A minimum payment per month is usually equal to 1/36th of the total amount out-

standing. May have annual fee as well as interest. Visa/MasterCard.

4. **Travel and entertainment card**   Usually fairly high limit, but companies monitor spending habits. Due in 30 days, no partial payments allowed except in exceptional circumstances where one may negotiate a temporary partial payment. American Express, Carte Blanche, and Diners Club.

5. **Installment loans**   For cars, home appliances. Usually for a set number of equal monthly payments, which include both principal and interest. Can be tied to a specific item and secured by the item. If you default, the item can be repossessed. Other times, installment loans are used as personal loans based on your income. They may have prepayment penalty of one to three months' interest, but could be more. Watch out for "Rule of '78," in which you can owe more than you borrowed for several years after loan is taken. Not recommended.

6. **Mortgages**   Usually for home or other real estate. Might be a second or third mortgage. Also for home improvement. Guaranteed by the property and property cannot be disposed of without repaying the mortgage. If you default, the property may revert to the mortgage holder. Mortgages now vary from between 5 and 30 years in length. Usually, a standard monthly payment combining principal and interest. With the new mortgages, there may be fixed payment

> only for a certain period, perhaps 3 to 5 years, and then a readjustment to reflect changing interest rates. Prepayment penalties vary depending on the type of mortgage. Can be up to 6 months' interest.

Let's say you've used the Five Steps method, and now you're trying to build your credit portfolio. Not all credit is created equal, neither in the eyes of the credit companies themselves nor in the eyes of other potential creditors who use existing credit as a measure of what you should get, so you'll want a mix of credit both for carrying out your activities and for building your credit portfolio.

The simplest credit cards to get and the ones that count the least are probably oil cards. Until very recently when some companies discontinued them, oil cards were very easy to get.

The corollary of ease of access is that the card has little merit as far as recommending you for other credit. In general, oil cards are not reported through credit reporting bureaus unless you default, and they are not much help in getting your next credit.

Department store cards are next. The easiest to get are from stores where the most affluent people shop. Sears and J. C. Penney's seem to be tough. Neiman-Marcus and Saks are much more receptive.

Their collection practices follow suit. If you fail to pay your Sears or Penney's bill, you'll hear about it very quickly, while Neiman-Marcus follows the "gentleman owes his tailor and pays him at the end of the year" collection philosophy. Department stores do report credit use to the credit bureau, although some stores report more frequently than others.

Next on the hierarchy of credit cards are bank cards, Visa

and MasterCard (formerly known as BankAmericard and MasterCharge). These two cards are keyed to having a checking or savings account in a particular institution, although this is certainly not required. As we've seen, bank cards represent one of the most solid forms of credit available today, and they will open other credit doors for you. If you don't have a bank card, you basically "have not arrived" in credit. As credit criteria have tightened in recent years, bank cards have become more frequently linked to having an account at the issuing institution. However, there was a time not very long ago when several large banks marketed bank cards nationally by mail.

Bank cards are reported on your credit report and usually you can pay them in part or whole.

At the top of the hierarchy of cards is the travel card. Contrary to popular opinion, American Express did not invent the travel card, although it now dominates the market. The Diners Club travel card was initiated by Alfred Bloomingdale in 1950. The familiar green American Express card didn't appear until 1958.

These cards offer the highest limits, so if possible you should have one for maximum flexiblity. The drawback is they are due in thirty days. Don't ever charge on Diners Club or American Express unless funds will be available to pay the bill.

Surprisingly, despite its marketing campaign emphasizing its value in "building your credit," American Express does not report to credit reporting agencies. Diners Club does. Correspondingly, American Express has an active collection department, since nonpayment won't stop you from getting other credit because no one except American Express would know.

Mortgage credit is the crème de la crème of credit because it can provide you with equity growth, tax shelter benefits, and positive cash flow.

Without mortgage access, until 1974 we women had difficulty entering the lucrative real estate market. Before that, the primary models for women's home ownership were spinster-hood, widowhood, and divorce. *The New York Times* recently reported that primarily as a result of the Equal Credit Opportunity Act, bolstered by changes in social attitudes, women's confidence, and the movement of women to better paying jobs, women buy one out of ten homes today, up from one out of sixteen in 1976. Women also buy one-third of the condominiums sold.

Home ownership can be an important means for you to take control of your life through control of your physical space, as well as offering financial advantages. The ultimate goal of your struggles with the credit system is to put you in a position to be able to afford and obtain a good mortgage whether for primary residence or for investment.

You should keep a careful eye on the mortgage market. Hold your money in reserve and don't buy emotionally. Wait until you see a major downward shift in prices and interest, and be ready to make an offer on a house that has been on the market for a bit, one with a motivated seller. Over the next few years, we will continue to see fluctuating mortgage rates. A smart buyer will be poised to take advantage of trends.

Which is preferable, a longer mortgage term or a shorter one? Go for the longest mortgage term or longest term on any credit that you can get, because you can always pay it off early with relatively little cost. The longer due date increases your own flexibility. Also, money decreases in value over time, so you'll be repaying any loan in less valuable money as time goes on.

Be realistic in your expectations, but don't take no for an answer too readily. Pursue credit systematically. Don't apply for credit if you haven't seen your credit report (or your husband's) recently, make sure you spell out your assets clearly, apply in person, and start close to home at your local bank.

Your best bet is to try first the "know-your-banker" method. If your banker is uncooperative, seriously consider moving your accounts elsewhere. Interview decision-makers in other institutions before you move your account, not after.

Use accounting truths, but don't lie. And don't spend money for someone to apply for credit for you. There aren't any secret methods other than the Five Steps plan outlined on page 110. And don't be tempted by ads offering to get credit for you for a fee.

To be ready, complete the sample application as your homework for this chapter.

7

Credit for Your Credit

The credit you get depends in large part on your credit report. If you know how credit reporting works, you may even be able to use the report to your credit advantage. But dealing with credit bureaus can be frustrating.

Credit bureaus are bureaucracies whose bread is buttered by the companies who hire them, not by consumers. Their profit is made from selling information about your private life to others. Despite their tremendous powers over consumers' lives, consumer control over them is limited to seeing one's own report, correcting it for errors, and inserting consumer comments when the report needs an explanation of past problems.

Here's the popular view of how the credit scenario works. You go down to the Main Street Emporium to open a charge account to buy a dress for a special occasion. The retailer asks you to fill out a credit application. On the application, you list three other department store charge accounts, a bank card, an oil card, one auto loan, and a home mortgage. You also reveal your place of employment, telephone number, and supervisor's name.

Then you wait while the Emporium supposedly calls each creditor on your application, right? Wrong—the application is designed to make you think that this is the way the process works.

But it isn't cost-effective even for a large retailer to check each detail on your credit application. Usually only one call is made, to a credit reporting bureau where a complete reading of your file is obtained. By paying a subscriber fee to such a credit reporting agency, the Emporium can easily check on how you have performed in the past.

Large retail stores often have direct access computer terminals of their own. This terminal flashes your credit file directly from the headquarters of the credit reporting agency to a computer screen in the Emporium's credit department. (That's how you can get such instant answers if you go in person under the Five Step plan.) The creditor can additionally order a written copy of your report, but may not bother.

Why must you fill out all that data on an application if the credit report has it too? By asking you to furnish the information, the Emporium has both a check on your truthfulness and a more accurate picture of your outstanding debts, since you will probably list accounts on your application that do not appear on your credit report. Since only creditors who subscribe to that particular credit bureau will be listed on the credit report, the creditor would never know about your accounts that don't show up on the credit bureau report unless you mention them.

But no matter how much data you have listed on your application, the Emporium's final credit decision will probably be made after one simple phone call to a credit reporting bureau, maybe with an additional call to your employer to verify income. Many larger employers will not give out income figures.

In this case the personnel office will usually refer the creditor directly back to your office. Thus, many consumers report that sometimes they, themselves, get calls from potential creditors to verify their own incomes!

Another false impression many consumers have is that the reporting agency gathers the information on its own. More often than not, a credit bureau merely keeps track of information provided to it by its own customers, your creditors. The Emporium, for example, would report back to the bureau on a regular basis, adding your track record to your credit bureau's files on you.

The credit bureau has a limited responsibility for the accuracy of the information it keeps. If a creditor reports incorrect information, it's not up to the agency to check it. You, the consumer, must correct the error by pointing the mistake out to the merchant.

The consumer has no say as to which bureau handles her credit file—her creditors do. Let's look at the case of Patricia Nicols to illustrate what happens to a consumer as a result of being ignored by "Big Brother."

Patricia Nicols had tried all the ordinary ploys to get credit and had invented a few of her own. She earned $22,000 a year, had no blemishes on her credit record, had paid several sizable loans off ahead of schedule and yet she had no credit record at TRW and couldn't get a Sears card or a Citicorp account without it. Her TRW record only showed inquiries by these two companies, both of whom said no.

Patricia had several excellent reference letters from credit unions. Ms. Nicols's arsenal even included a banker's letter, although many banks stopped issuing them about the time they started issuing bank cards. These organizations subscribed to bureaus other than TRW or didn't subscribe at all in order to "protect the confidentiality" of accounts. Hoping to get these references listed, Ms. Nicols decided to forward the letters to TRW.

TRW's reply clearly spells out the problem consumers have with the credit reporting system.

The information we have in your credit file is supplied to us only by our "subscribers" and from selected court records. By the term "subscribers" we mean those credit grantors who have contracted with us to use our reporting service. As part of that contract, these "subscribers" agree to inform us of the latest status of the accounts they open. For example, your bank might report a loan which they granted you for a car. In the course of that loan, if payments are not made as agreed, we would be automatically notified. We would again be notified when the loan is subsequently paid. Our "subscribers" think of us as an up-to-date, constantly changing source of credit information.

If we add to your file credit information not reported by our subscribers, it will quickly become outdated. The subscribers will know this information is not constantly being kept current, and consequently, they probably will pay little or no attention to the information, thus, no real benefit will result from adding this information to your file.

Although we are one of the major credit reporting agencies in the nation, we do not pretend to always have your entire credit history, nor do we make such a claim to our subscribers. We try to help the credit grantors (and you) by providing them with lists of those subscribers who use our service. Our subscribers are aware that our file may not contain all your past or present credit accounts, and they should keep this in mind when evaluating your credit application and your TRW Credit Data file. In the future it may be of benefit to you when applying for credit to list on the application your other credit accounts.

The last sentence, an apparent non sequitur, tells the tale. Ms. Nicols had just listed her "other credit accounts" but they weren't subscribers to TRW, therefore neither Sears nor Citicorp would give her credit for them. The application which, in the words of Citicorp, had been "reviewed carefully" had, in fact, not been. A TRW report was requested, but once no record was found for this consumer, that was the end of the process.

Before anything else, you must determine which agency or agencies hold your records and you must see your credit report. But even finding a large company like TRW is not always simple. When I lived in Boston some time ago, I looked for TRW Credit Data in the Boston Yellow Pages under "Credit Reporting Agencies," but there was no listing. By calling TRW headquarters in Los Angeles I found that TRW was the predominant bureau in the area, but it was based in a suburb and wasn't listed in the Boston Yellow Pages.

One of the best ways to find out which bureau your potential or current creditors use is simply to ask the creditors themselves. Otherwise, you may ask a local banker or business person.

As soon as you have located your file, begin work on getting a look at it. Your task may not be easy. Credit agencies are often bureaucratic and thus frustrating to deal with.

Prior to the enactment of the consumer laws, consumers had absolutely outrageous experiences with credit reporting bureaus. A consumer had no way of knowing if a credit report had damaging information, and there was no way to correct errors. Thanks to the passage of the Consumer Credit Protection Act in 1968 and the addition of the Fair Credit Reporting Act in 1970, horror stories about the credit reporting industry have diminished. Today, consumers have a legal right to view their credit report at the credit reporting bureau for free, but the bureau is not required by federal law to give you a copy of your report. Some states, like New York, have laws that do require it. Luckily, the more responsible agencies will now supply duplicates for a fee. (I used to say "small fee," but since the law was enacted the fee has climbed from $4 to about $8.)

But federal law does require that the consumer be given access to her credit report without charge if she has been denied credit based on information in the report. Under this circumstance, you may contact your credit agency within thirty days and have a free look, either in person or by mail if the creditor so permits.

A few years ago, I decided to go down to the Orange County, California, headquarters of TRW to get my own credit report. I was in the middle of a mortgage transaction and I learned that there was something that needed correction in my credit report. Before discussing the report with the bank, I wanted to know precisely what was wrong.

I appeared at TRW and was told that the earliest appointment I could make for a credit check was in about ten days. In a week the opportunity to buy the property would be lost, so I persisted. In my opinion, this appointment procedure violated the spirit of the Fair Credit Reporting Act, which provides that credit information be granted in person to a consumer with proper identification. I told TRW so, and I saw my report. As it turned out, the mistake in the report was the creditor's, not mine. I would have lost a good deal had I waited a week to discover that error.

While at the bureau, I saw many consumers, some who had driven an hour from downtown Los Angeles to get to TRW's suburban office in Orange County, being told to call for an appointment. Since they didn't know the law, they were resigned to making yet another trip to this, the closest bureau serving Los Angeles.

This experience taught me the value of reviewing your

credit report before you need credit. Call your credit reporting bureau and determine whether you can order a copy and for what fee. Write a letter providing your name, address (list all addresses for the past five years if you've moved), social security number, any names that you may have previously used to get credit, and enclose the fee. (See the Sample Credit Report Order, page 138.)

Always keep a photocopy of your order letter. Although most credit reporting agencies claim that they process consumer requests within twenty-four to forty-eight hours, I have worked with consumers who had to wait as long as three months to receive a return copy of their report. If you have not received the report within about ten days, I recommend forwarding the bureau a copy of your request letter and writing in red letters across the front NOT RECEIVED.

If your bureau doesn't supply written reports, make an appointment and go review the details. The law states that you be permitted to take one other person with you. If financial meetings make you nervous, by all means take a friend with you.

A credit report is written in computer language with many abbreviations. Unfortunately that makes it all the more difficult for the average consumer to detect mistakes. Look at the back of your credit report for the fine print. You'll find initials for every conceivable variety of financial interaction. These abbreviations are your key to decoding your report.

Consumer "ratings" don't work like Dun and Bradstreet business and institutional letter gradings. The credit bureau simply records fairly detailed information about credit activity in your various accounts. Your potential creditor does the interpreting based on the raw data. For example, if you've been late paying an account, your credit bureau will record the details of the delinquency (balance due and amount past due).

SAMPLE CREDIT REPORT ORDER

From: Date:

To: (Credit Bureau)

_____

_____

_____

_____

Dear Sir or Madam:
   Please send me a copy of my credit profile. Following is the pertinent information:

Name: _____

Social Security: _____

Birthdate: _____

Present Residence: _____

_____

Past Residences (the last five years): _____

_____

                        _____

                                Signature

Check one:
__   Check enclosed
__   I have been denied credit within the past 30 days as a result of information from your credit file, or there is an error in the information in my credit file.

Other columns may give the credit limit for each account, and the date each account was last verified. Some credit reports will give a complete reporting for every month, but variation in reporting is common. A "POS" (positive) account profile together with a reliable payment record over some months guarantees a sound rating.

In addition to the standard designations of "individual" or "joint" accounts, the Equal Credit Opportunity Act provides for the creation of a "user" designation. This category, as we saw in chapter 4, was added to give a woman credit for accounts she uses regularly, although the account is actually recorded in her husband's name. Sometimes there's a separate column to indicate the Equal Credit Opportunity Act "user" category.

If a mistake has been made by the reporting agencies, they are required by law to correct the information. Also keep in mind, however, that the agency is merely gathering information from your creditors. If Robinson's department store makes an error in reporting on your account, you must let the store know that you expect a change. It's wise to recheck your credit report soon after you've requested a correction. If you wait until you actually want credit, it will be too late to get it done in time.

Let's turn to the sample credit report of Mrs. Lee Shigemura, a consumer who attended one of our credit seminars. (See page 140.)

Going from left to right across the page, you'll see the "Account Profile." In this column, one of three abbreviations is used: "POS" for positive, "NEG" for negative, and "NON" for not evaluated, as it is generally viewed by credit grantors. You'll note that Mrs. Shigemura had not had any problems with her Robinson's account and so the account profile shows "POS."

In the next column to the right, immediately under the "Subscriber Name," which in this case is Robinson's, is the ab-

TRW CREDIT DATA UPDATED CREDIT PROFILE CONFIDENTIAL

PAGE	DATE	TIME	PORT	H/V		
1	12/10/84	1H/4/:35	HK20	D42	MRS. SHIGEMURA	20-235117/8

ACCOUNT PROFILE	SUBSCRIBER NAME / COURT NAME			SUBSCRIBER # COURT CODE	ASSN CODE			ACCOUNT NUMBER/DOCKET		PAYMENT PROFILE NUMBER OF MONTHS PRIOR TO BALANCE DATE
POS NON NEG	STATUS COMMENT	DATE REPORTED/ INQUIRY	DATE OPENED	TYPE	TERMS	AMOUNT	BALANCE	BALANCE DATE	AMOUNT PAST DUE	1 2 3 4 5 6 7 8 9 10 11 12
A	J W ROBINSONS			174209	2			697421		
	CURR ACCT	12-84	10-78	CHG	REV	$200	10	12-1-84		CCCCCCCCCCCC
----END										

breviation "CURR ACCT," which stands for "current account." This simply indicates that the account has not been closed and is still active.

To the right again, we see the date 12/84, which is the date the account was last reported on. The next date, 10/78, refers to the month and year the account was first opened. To the creditor reading this report, this information indicates that the account has been open for approximately six years and that the last information received on it was in December 1984.

The next column to the right, "Subscriber Code #/ Court Code Type," refers to the subscriber, Robinson's, not the consumer, Mrs. Shigemura.

Under the next column, "Assn Code Terms," you'll see the abbreviation "REV," which stands for "revolving," and describes the type of charge account Mrs. Shigemura enjoys at Robinson's.

The column "Account Number/Docket" is the number assigned to Mrs. Shigemura's account by the credit grantor or court. The "Balance Date" and "Amount Past Due" are of particular interest to you because if you've ever been late in paying an account, it is here that the details of the delinquency will be recorded. The balance date shows the date the balance was reported and the actual amount past due on the balance date, if any.

According to Mrs. Shigemura's record, she owes nothing and there is nothing past due. The "Amount" indicates her credit limit of $200. As of the "Balance Date," 12/1/84, she owes $10 more.

Finally, in the far right-hand column, you'll see a "Payment Profile." Under each of the twelve numbers listed, you'll notice C's have been recorded to indicate that Mrs. Shigemura's account was current each of the twelve months preceding the 12/84 reporting date.

Having glanced over Mrs. Shigemura's entire report, we can quickly establish her overall performance level. Her "POS" account profile, together with her payment profile over the last several months, indicates her basic credit history is a good one.

Next, we compared Mrs. Shigemura's report from TRW and another large bureau, Trans Union, to Mr. Shigemura's reports from the same two bureaus.

Although there were considerable variations between the two agencies in credit they reported for Mr. Shigemura, both of them did better for him than for Mrs. Shigemura (Table 9).

Table 9. A MARRIED WOMAN'S MISSING CREDIT

Mrs. Shigemura	Mr. Shigemura	Mrs. Shigemura	Mr. Shigemura
TRW	*TRW*	*Trans Union*	*Trans Union*
		Security Pacific National Bank	Security Pacific National Bank
	Bank of America		Bank of America
			J.C. Penney
		May Co.	May Co.
	Bullocks		Bullocks
Robinson's	Robinson's	Robinson's	Robinson's
	Sears	Sears	Sears
			Texaco
	Macy's		
	Broadway (regular)	Broadway	
	Broadway (home appliance)		

Any consumer has every expectation that two credit reports will reflect the same information about herself. Imagine how surprised Mrs. Shigemura was when she learned that many accounts for which she has a credit card and which she uses regularly were not listed at all on either of her two reports. What happened to Bullocks? Macy's? Sears?

The moral of all this: If you are a woman who has been married for some years, particularly if you were married prior to 1977 and the Equal Credit Opportunity Act took effect, you might very well find a good portion of what should be on your credit report noted only on your husband's.

You would think that opening an account in your name only would solve your problem of a disappearing credit record, but it won't necessarily. Mrs. Shigemura applied for a Visa card in her own name precisely for the purpose of establishing credit for herself. Still, both her credit reports failed even to show a record of her own Visa account, instead listing it under Mr. Shigemura's name (Bank of America entry).

Mrs. Shigemura's case demonstrates two key points: First, order your credit report yearly to be sure all of the cards for which you are responsible are on it. If you are married, you can save yourself a lot of time by requesting your husband's report when you order your own credit report. But order separately, as I don't recommend informing the credit bureau of your marriage until you've had a chance to check his report.

Second, Mrs. Shigemura's history clearly illustrates the residual presence of sex discrimination in credit reporting. I have never yet seen a man's credit report that failed to show accounts that were only in his name, while his wife's report failed to show all her own accounts, as well as theirs. This difference is a holdover from the days when files were manila folders, not computerized records, and a wife's file was literally placed inside her husband's.

143

There are other typical mistakes that creditors make in the credit file of a married woman. Often even if you have requested "joint" accounts, your record shows only "user's" status.

You may not find a great distinction between "joint" and "user," but your potential creditors most certainly do. On a user account, you are not liable for the financial obligation; in a joint account, if the other person does not pay the bill, you will have to. Contractually liable account holders are protected against reapplication requirements, change in terms, or termination of the account on the basis of age, retirement, or a change in marital status, whereas authorized users are not. (See chapter 4, no. 26.)

Let the creditor(s) in question know that you expect a change if you find these kinds of omissions and mistakes in your record. Your request should specify that you are writing under the provisions of the Equal Credit Opportunity Act. Look at the Sample Credit Reporting Request, page 145. I recommend photocopying as many of these form letters as you have accounts and keeping them where you pay your bills. Then as you pay the bill just fill in the pertinent information and send the letter along. In a month or two, you'll have your reporting requests in.

Creditors have ninety days to comply with your request to report an account properly, although local stores and merchants often don't understand their obligations under federal credit laws. So if you don't receive a response, send a photostatic copy of your original letter with big red writing across it: YOUR 90-DAY LEGAL LIMIT UNDER THE EQUAL CREDIT OPPORTUNITY ACT IS OVER. PLEASE REPLY BY RETURN MAIL. You may eventually have to call the store manager and demand action, but, whatever you do, recheck your report at the bureau by writing for another copy or follow up in person to be sure the credit now appears there.

SAMPLE CREDIT REPORTING REQUEST

From: Date:

_____   _____

_____

_____

Dear Credit Manager:

Please report all information concerning the account listed below in both of our names, as provided for by the Equal Credit Opportunity Act, Regulation B.

Name: _____

Spouse's Name: _____

Name in which account is listed (name on the billing statement):

_____

Account Number: _____

_____

Signature of either spouse

Let's look at a consumer with an active credit life and a full credit report.

A professional woman in her mid-thirties, Ms. Williamson has married for the second time. She keeps her birth name for her credit and her professional life. She only uses her current married name for social purposes, which makes it easier to track her credit history.

When her most recent credit report was issued, Ms. Williamson owned three pieces of property and had a total of five mortgages—not an uncommon occurrence in California. The total of all her mortgages amounted to more than $300,000, so she had a monthly carrying charge in excess of $3,000. But only one of her mortgages was reflected in her credit report. Why weren't the other mortgages recorded?

From my research, I've learned that your mortgage credit is usually examined only when you are buying other property. Unlike creditors who rely on credit bureaus exclusively, potential mortgage creditors also make individual contact with other mortgage lenders. Since mortgages are most frequently against your home, lenders assume that you'll protect your largest investment if possible. If you don't, your foreclosure will appear in court records and thus on your report.

Because mortgages aren't reported, Ms. Williamson enjoys a good credit rating that erroneously reflects low debt obligations.

Mortgages were not the only credit information not reflected in Ms. Williamson's credit bureau report. She had a $12,000 auto loan with Wells Fargo Bank. With a car in her life, surely Ms. Williamson has an oil card; yet the report shows none. Oil companies tend not to report accounts unless they are negative.

Ms. Williamson also has an American Express card. As previously noted, the only relationship American Express has with the credit reporting system is in obtaining information about you. American Express does not feed back into the system, so your American Express account will not help—or hinder—your credit rating.

Reporting patterns can be used to advantage in a financial crisis. (See chapter 9.) By knowing which accounts to let slip and which ones she must pay, Ms. Williamson has preserved her credit rating beautifully.

It's also a simple matter to omit from credit applications

accounts that you know are not on record at the credit reporting bureau. Such omissions easily improve the looks of credit application by lowering the ratio of debt to income. While omitting accounts from your credit applications is not recommended, you should know that selective omissions are often the very reason why some people get credit while others in the same financial position do not.

Finally, let's look at a credit consumer who let an unpaid bill for $92 cost her several thousand dollars of lost credit.

Sarah Mount, a single woman earning $18,000 a year, has few entries in her credit report and those she has are negative. Her Sears account has been 120 days past due, her Lechmere's account 180 days past due, and Jordan's has been "charged off" as a business loss for tax purposes by the creditor. Of her available credit, totaling $600, she has overcharged her Sears account by $50 and her Jordan's by $42. In effect, Ms. Mount has ruined her credit because of late payments amounting to no more than $92, less than one week's salary.

Ms. Mount is now unable to get a car loan. She earns decent money, has relatively few debts, but she's handled the ones she has poorly. During a serious emotional crisis, she was too depressed to pay her bills. At the time we talked, the pile still cluttered her desk. Since she had the means to make good on her outstanding obligations, my advice to Sarah Mount was to straighten out her credit rating before attempting to incur any new debts.

Once her bills are paid off, will there be a way to clean up her record? It's very difficult, though not impossible.

Like Mount, Williamson once had trouble obtaining a car loan. When she was turned down, Ms. Williamson learned that her credit report was blemished. Her former husband had owed a tax debt that the state had levied against her. She found that even though the state tax board had written TRW about the mistake, the entry hadn't been removed from her report. Therefore, she prepared to take legal action. In the meantime she inserted the one-hundred-word consumer comment that the law mandates consumer reporting bureaus must include if requested. Her comment explained the facts.

The next time she needed credit, Williamson forewarned the creditor about the lien. With the help of the consumer comment and her own verbal explanation before the creditor received a copy of the report, she was able to make an end run around the problem and obtain her loan.

If you've tarnished your own credit rating, you can follow Williamson's example. First communicate with the subscriber who reported the problem, reserving the consumer comment as a last resort.

Mrs. Bremen is a good example of someone who managed to "undo" her past mistakes. Having lost her husband, job, and health within a period of months, she had stretched her credit beyond the limit and couldn't avoid having thirty- and sixty-day late accounts. One creditor even suspended her card. But when Mrs. Bremen recovered, she paid her bills on time for a year, then wrote on expensive stationery to each creditor. She reminded her creditors that she had contacted them when the problem first occurred, and referred them to her recent record of prompt payment. Mrs. Bremen then made a simple request: Would the creditor remove the negative information, which covered a relatively brief time over a year ago? Sure enough, all the creditors complied and she once again has an exemplary credit record.

Even in tight economic times, this tactic is definitely worth a try. Consider calling the credit managers in the particular stores or companies and asking them for the same courtesy. A "deep cleaning" may do your own credit report a world of good.

If it doesn't work, don't be discouraged. By law, negative information can only be kept for seven years, unless it is about bankruptcy, which can be retained for ten. You can still insert your consumer comment, and as the years pass, your potential creditors will view older scars less harshly.

No one can make a creditor extend credit, and there's presently no way to force a creditor to check each reference individually. If a consumer's reports are scattered between bureaus, she's out of luck. What's the solution?

First, creditors ought to be required to make a good faith effort to check accounts individually, provided you've given written permission to do so.

Secondly, if credit bureaus are to continue to have the power over our financial lives they currently enjoy, consumers ought to demand and get the ability to have cross-checking done by them on accounts reported to other bureaus. A one-time entry showing substantial paid accounts would certainly be taken seriously by the creditor.

Soon all our financial transactions will be electronic, and most of them will be centralized in our home computer files. If the one-stop financial services succeed, checking our financial records will only require one stop, too. Shouldn't we start protecting ourselves now by demanding some control over the reporting process?

For the present, review the Credit Report Checklist below and follow its recommendations.

CREDIT REPORT CHECKLIST

1. Find major credit bureau(s) in your area.

2. Order credit report or go in person to see it.

3. If married, order husband's report.

4. Review report for errors vis-à-vis payment of bills or personal identifying facts (year of birth, marital status, etc.).

5. If accounts are missing from your report for reasons other than marital status, including a recent move, ask the credit reporting bureau whether you can pay a fee and have them added. There's no legal provision for this, so it will be up to individual credit bureaus.

6. Review for omissions of joint and user accounts or accounts for which you are liable by virtue of state property laws. Reminder for residents of community property states: By definition you're liable for your husband's accounts, so they should be on your report.

7. Request credit managers of each account to make corrections and additions. Use Sample Credit Reporting Request, page 145, as a guide.

8. Recheck your credit report after ninety days to see if your request was honored. If not, remind creditors they are in violation of the Equal Credit Opportunity Act, Regulation B, Sect. 202.10(c), for not responding in ninety days and of the Equal Credit Opportunity Act, Regulation B, Sect. 202.10(a), if marital accounts aren't reported as requested. (See chapter 4.)

9. If creditors refuse to adjust past negative reports, insert your one-hundred-word "consumer comment" explaining your side of the situation.

Part Four

MAXIMIZING CREDIT

8

Making Money
with Credit

Once you have a good credit base, it's time to put it to work, not necessarily for getting rich, but certainly for staying solvent.

In the modern world of finance, the taking and giving of credit is big business. The average American corporation can't grow without credit and neither can you.

Having credit is not enough. You have to know how to use it. Every investment decision involves three basic components: cash flow, tax shelter benefits, and equity growth. Credit and capital, or what's known as the two investor basics, debt and equity, fit together in this picture to provide the tools for maximizing all three.

Department store accounts, bank cards, and travel cards provide financial identity, some tax benefits, and convenience, but their real value to you is that they allow you access to the money-makers of credit. Mortgage loans are the entrée for most of us. Mortgages allow you to take advantage of the tax benefits, leverage, and equity growth of real estate, while business loans can help you escape the salary trap and continuing corporate resistance to women at the top.

TAX ADVANTAGES OF CREDIT

1. Example of credit-related items on which interest is deductible:

   • Bank cards
   • Department store accounts
   • Airline tickets if paid on extended payments
   • Interest on bank loans, including business loans
   • Mortgage interest

2. How to figure the value of the deduction:

   • Find your effective (marginal) tax bracket (% at which you are taxed after taking all deductions). To figure, check last year's tax return to get the amount you paid in federal taxes. Be sure to include amounts withheld. Divide the annual amount of your federal taxes by your gross income. The resulting figure, expressed as a percent, is your current effective tax bracket.
   • Add up all the interest charges
   • Multiply dollars interest times marginal tax bracket equals actual cash savings
     $_____ × _____% = $_____
     Interest × Tax Bracket = Cash Savings

Debt is expensive in today's high interest times but even when you include interest, you can make money using other people's money. Some people are so good at structuring deals, they achieve 100 percent leverage, making all their money on other people's. The usual model involves using some capital or equity of your own and sharing the risk with the lender. For example, for mortgages, ordinarily you'd have to come up with

20 percent down, and in business, 50 percent is the rule. To look at one example, mortgages, you earn on your equity or down payment, and on the bank's loan too. If housing prices and interest rates rise, you have the use of the lender's money at a lower price over a long time. Some of this advantage has been eroded in recent years with high, variable interest loans, but leverage can still work its magic, enabling you to control large assets with your "lever" or smaller down payment.

Whether you are a big business or an individual, the trick is deciding how to achieve "optimum capital structure" by finding the mix of debt and equity you can afford. Part of the equation always includes calculating the tax impact of debt. Our tax provisions make interest payments deductible. To see if you can afford to carry a major debt like a mortgage or a business loan, you have to calculate the exact tax consequences. To continue the example for property, in addition to interest, property taxes are deductible. If your property is a rental, you'll have additional tax benefits flowing from depreciation.

In this chapter, we'll explore how these principles worked for one woman, Melissa Hilton, who made money on her credit, and let the government, through tax provisions, share the cost.

In the rarefied real estate market of West Los Angeles, Melissa Hilton stands out as a woman who knew what she wanted, went after it, and got it. She moved from a $400-a-month apartment to a $300,000 home in the blink of an eye.

Not all of us can do what Melissa did, yet her use of credit illustrates what's possible. Melissa's informed use of her tax savings to make her mortgage affordable is a model of good credit management, and the principles she took advantage of apply equally whether you are Melissa Hilton or a woman in a town where the average house is $30,000, not $300,000.

As a single attorney, Melissa earned $45,000, which then put her close to the 45 percent bracket when she bought her home. Now rates are somewhat lower. (See Table 10 for current tax rates.) At age twenty nine, she was blessed with high income and yet she was too young to have acquired much in the way of tax deductions. She wanted to buy a home but even with her high income, in the West Los Angeles real estate market she couldn't qualify for the type of house she wanted.

Table 10. YOUR APPROXIMATE EFFECTIVE TAX BRACKET

Single		Married (Filing Joint)	
Taxable Income OF	*Is Taxed AT*	*Taxable Income OF*	*Is Taxed AT*
3,400	4%	5,500	4%
4,400	5%	7,600	6%
6,500	8%	11,900	9%
8,500	10%	16,000	11%
10,900	11%	20,200	12%
12,900	12%	24,600	14%
15,000	13%	29,900	16%
18,200	15%	35,200	18%
23,500	18%	45,800	21%
28,800	20%	60,000	25%
34,100	22%	85,600	30%
41,500	25%	109,400	33%
55,300	29%	162,400	39%

Tax rates have changed annually over recent years to implement the 1981 Economic Recovery Tax Act (ERTA and the Deficit Reduction Act of 1984); therefore, tax brackets are approximate and each dollar above the amount cited is taxed at a different rate. Check for current tax rates with the IRS or review your last return and use the formula in Tax Advantages of Credit, p. 154.

Using the rule of thumb that the price of the house purchased should equal no more than 2.5 times annual income, she would qualify for a house in the $112,500 price range. In West Los Angeles, houses at this price disappeared from the market during the late seventies real estate boom—and they show no signs of returning.

Melissa purchased a house for $293,000 with a thirty-year fixed loan at 12 percent. The monthly payments for "PITI" (Principal, Interest, Taxes, and Insurance) were $2,707. Using the lender rule of thumb of four times housing payment to equal monthly income, to qualify, Melissa would have needed $9,052 per month income, far higher than her $3,750 per month. Also, with her high tax bracket and young single life-style, she had accumulated no savings for the down payment.

Her solution: She was able to make the purchase by splitting the house with a partner, who provided the down payment. She took advantage of the tax shelter benefits of home ownership, which she also shared with her partner. As part of a new job package, she persuaded her employer to be that partner.

When the house is sold, she'll have to return her partner's down payment from her share of the profits. In the meantime, she will have benefited from tax savings and participation in equity growth. She has leveraged her money 100 percent, since she put nothing down, and reduced her effective tax bracket.

Now let's look at the Analysis of Home Ownership Costs, page 158, showing exactly how the tax benefits work to reduce the cash cost of her home for Melissa. On line 1, the total purchase price is $293,000. On line 2, the approximately 25 percent down payment is $73,000. Subtracting line 2 from line 1 leaves $220,000, the amount to be financed. At 12 percent for thirty years, monthly payments of principal and interest are $2,263. Monthly property taxes and insurance costs bring monthly out-of-pocket cost of $2,707, before considering the tax advantages.

ANALYSIS OF
HOME OWNERSHIP COSTS

Basic Facts	MELISSA HILTON'S	YOURS
1. Sale Price of Home:	$293,000	_____
2. Cash Down:	73,000	_____
3. Loan:	220,000	_____
4. Monthly Payments, principal and interest:	2,263	_____
5. Monthly Deposit for property taxes:	244	_____
6. Monthly Deposit for insurance, approximately:	200	_____
7. Total Monthly Payment (lines 4, 5, and 6)	2,707	_____

Expense Items for Income Tax Purposes

8. First month's interest:*	2,195	_____
9. Monthly property tax deposit:	244	_____
10. Total Deductions: (line 8 plus line 9)	2,439	_____
11. Tax Bracket: (See Table 10.)	×45%	_____
12. Tax Savings per month: (line 11 times line 10)	1,098	_____

Total After-Tax Cost:

13. Total Monthly Payment: (line 7)	2,707	_____

14. Less Tax Savings: (line 12)   <u>1,098</u>   _____

15. Effective Monthly Cost: (line 7
minus line 12)   <u>1,609</u>   _____

16. Subtract equity,* which is being gained monthly: (line 4 mi-
nus line 8)   68   _____

17. Actual Monthly Cost: <u>1,541</u>   _____

*Interest amount decreases by small amount each month and equity increases by the same proportion.

The interest both on the loan and on the property taxes is tax deductible, but to see what part of a monthly payment is deductible you have to separate the interest from the total payment.

Mortgage loans are constructed so that a level or standard payment is made each month, but in reality the percentage of the total payment that is interest shifts with each payment. In the first years of a loan, most of the payments are interest. In later years, more is paid into retirement of the debt or to principal.

To see the exact relationship between interest and principal in a loan, you'd have to consult an amortization table or look at your loan payment schedule. For example, see Table 11 on the following page for interest for a thirty-year loan at 12 percent. As you can see from the Analysis of Home Ownership Costs, page 158, a mortgage provides more in tax deductions during the first half of its life. Since about 97 percent of Melissa's payments in the first year will be to interest, I've multiplied line 4 by 97 percent to get the figure on line 8, or $2,195 total monthly interest. Since property taxes are also deductible from federal income tax, they are added to interest for a total of $2,439 in deductible items (line 10).

Table 11. LOAN AMORTIZATION

Age of Loan	Percent That Is Interest
(Years)	*(%)*
1	96.7
5	96
10	91
15	84.6
20	71.7
25	48
30	6

These figures are for a 30-year fixed loan at 12% interest. The rate will vary according to the length of the loan and the interest rate.

To establish the cash value of these amounts to Melissa, the deductible items are multiplied by her marginal tax bracket, or the tax she'd pay on her next dollar, assuming she has already taken her other deductions. To see her bracket, we looked in Table 10. Since Melissa is in the 45 percent bracket, meaning each dollar she earns is taxed 45 cents, taking these items off her gross income will save her 45 cents on the dollar, or 45 percent. The savings reflected in line 12 are $2,439 × 45 percent or $1,098 (line 14).

To see the value of these savings in cash flow terms, we take the total monthly cost of her new house of $2,707, subtract the $1,098 in tax savings for an effective monthly cost of $1,609.

Finally, since some equity is being paid in each month through debt retirement, we can subtract that amount (line 16) to see the actual monthly cost (line 17).

The results in line 15 and line 17 provide compelling evidence of the cash value of credit when coupled with the tax benefits.

Even with these savings, Melissa could neither qualify under the usual lender rules of thumb nor could she afford the effects of such high payments on her cash flow. The approximately $1,609 per month effective cost times four equaled $6,436, still well above her monthly income of $3,750. But dividing the effective cost in half, or $804.50, made it affordable. Four times $804.50 equals $3,218, well below Melissa's monthly income.

Even with a partner Melissa still felt financially pressed. When we met, her biggest problem was that she had not adjusted her withholding forms, even though she was now entitled to many more deductions.

Like many taxpayers, she thought of her W-4 exemptions as equal to the number of dependents, so the government was still taking its bite monthly while she was making the higher monthly house payment, much of which is deductible. Even though a refund would come at the end of the year, the failure to adjust her W-4 had affected her cash flow.

In order to get the immediate advantage of tax shelter benefits created by her mortgage, Melissa had to figure out her correct withholding. As a single person with no dependents, she had one exemption. But with literally thousands of dollars of annual interest, she could claim increased standard deductions.

To calculate these, we took her monthly tax deduction now available from the house of $2,439 (page 158, line 10) and multiplied by twelve to reach an annual figure of $29,268 in additional tax deductions. Since her employer was entitled to half the benefit of half of the deductions for his part of the interest and property tax, she had to divide the total deductions of $29,268 in half, for a total of $14,634 or almost $15,000 in new tax deductions for herself.

The IRS provides that for each $1,000 in new deductions you can add one "standard deduction" to your W-4. Melissa divided the $14,634 by $1,000 to come up with a figure of $14.63 additional standard deductions. When she added this figure to the deduction she is entitled to as a single taxpayer, she now had $15.63 in deductions.

The personnel officer in Melissa's firm pointed out that if she took more than fourteen standard deductions, the firm was required to report to the IRS, which in turn would require documentation to support her claim.

To be on the safe side, Melissa opted for taking fourteen deductions. Upon reviewing her taxes after the first year of home ownership, she could make adjustments. If with fourteen deductions she still overpaid taxes and received a refund, then she would go ahead and increase her deductions.

Melissa's experience introduced her firsthand to concepts like cash flow, tax shelter benefits, equity growth, and leverage that she'd learned in law school. Let's see how she—and you—can use some related concepts to make an investment gained through credit and taxes grow further, too. These include liquidity, the time value of money, opportunity cost, and risk.

To look at liquidity, let's assume that the value of Melissa's house appreciated by $50,000. To realize that growth, she would have to sell her house, so this investment is less liquid than putting the same money in a money market account, where she could immediately turn both principal and interest to cash.

An additional factor, the time value of money, makes borrowed money attractive. If I offered to give you $100 today or $100 ten years from now, which would you choose? Almost everyone will answer, "Now," because all of us have an innate understanding of the time value of money.

Net present value (NPV) expresses that understanding in business terms. Let's say you wanted to get that same $100 today, but it's owed to you in ten years. How much less would you take for that $100 obligation if you could have the money today?

Your answer is equal to the net present value of that money, and to arrive at that answer you reduced or "discounted" that money.

When interest is high, you'd discount the money more, because the value of borrowed money is higher. In low interest times, the discount would be lower since the money would earn less if you put it to other uses.

In most standard financial texts, including accounting references, you can find tables to calculate the net present value of $1.00 for any discount figure you care to apply. Table 12 shows an example at 10 percent.

Table 12. THE TIME VALUE OF MONEY

Present Value of $1.00

Year	Discount rate 10%
1	.909
2	.826
3	.751
4	.683
5	.621
6	.564
7	.513

The difference between the investment you select and other possible uses is the "opportunity cost." It's the price you pay for following one plan and not the others. Any time you decide to invest in a particular direction, you are forgoing another.

Whether Melissa's investment proves wise in financial

terms compared to her opportunity cost will depend in part on how the real estate market does and in part on whether her property has unanticipated additional costs such as repairs.

The unanswerables form her risk. Every investment involves risk. Depending upon the nature of the undertaking and how the debt and equity are structured, you can lose just the amount of your down payment or possibly other financial resources. The worst case is to lose it all in bankruptcy. Finding your own risk tolerance and the balance between risk and stasis involves putting in careful thought. No one wants to lose money, but some risk is necessary to make it.

Melissa's case shows how a young professional woman applied her credit savvy and took advantage of her tax deductions to put money into a property that would grow in value. Her tax bill has been reduced from $20,250 to just over $13,000 annually. What she pays in interest would have gone straight to Uncle Sam. Instead it goes to the bank in interest (see how the tax system benefits bankers?). The difference to Melissa is that she owns her home. If the real estate market rises, through equity growth she will have made money on other people's money —both the bank's and the U.S. Treasury's.

If the market doesn't grow, Melissa has shifted the burden of monthly expense from taxes to interest and will still benefit over the long run, because she will eventually own the home.

Her story illustrates how credit works in tandem with the tax codes to the benefit of those who use them.

If your eyes are starting to glaze over at the thought of the intricacies of balancing debt and equity in the context of the tax system, think about the consequences of not making these trade-offs. As women, we need to use our financial clout to create a secure base for ourselves. Just when we were finally able to get credit and enter the lucrative real estate market, housing prices zoomed out of sight. In more recent times, real estate has experienced a slight downturn because of continued high interest rates, but times will change again. Do you know when to act?

To see, do the exercise on page 166 and see how you would fare if you bought a home either alone or with a partner. If you own a home now, check out your tax benefits by including your real-life figures. Even if you think you'd never consider buying property, seeing the relationship between mortgage interest and taxes will help you structure any investment you may consider.

As you're working along, you might ask yourself this question: Why is it that our tax structure provides such big breaks for the use of credit?

If people understood that taxpayers who don't own property are subsidizing those who do (the way you should understand it now), do you think they'd continue to be in favor of these tax provisions? What about the fact that so few women were allowed to buy houses until ten years ago? If few women understood these provisions because we had so little practical experience with them, and fewer still were able to act on that understanding, no wonder we've been behind financially.

Now let me pose one more question. Let's take as an example the tax treatment afforded child care, an important subject to many working women. Why is interest deductible dollar for dollar whereas even with the new "liberal" provisions, child care has a maximum tax credit of $1,400, and to qualify for the maximum you must have four children in day care? Women who are caught in the cycle of poverty and welfare, and even working middle-class women, find child care is the first item they must have and can't afford. Why not allow child care deductions to work like housing interest so women could have the chance to catch up?

Businesses use credit and the tax structure to maximize

profits and preserve capital. Women should also use this powerful set of tools and even work to change them to benefit us further.

Exercise

Question: How could you save money by investing your taxes?

1. If you have a mortgage now, do the analysis of home ownership costs to calculate your tax savings. You'll need to do some fact gathering before you start.

   Look up or ask your lender for your total mortgage amount, the interest rate, the number of years of the original mortgage, and the number of years it has to run. These last two pieces of information can be used to calculate what percent of your monthly payments are interest and what percent apply to principal or equity build-up.

   To get a very rough idea, you can use the percentage in Table 11, but remember, the percentages that are interest will vary according to the length of the loan and the interest rate.

   To see what portion of your current monthly payment is interest, multiply by the approximate percent in Table 11 according to the age of the loan. This will give you line 8 to use for the analysis. Subtract the interest from line 4, total monthly payment, and you'll have line 16, the equity being paid.

2. If you have no mortgage now, fill out the analysis to project how a home purchase in your price range would affect your tax picture. Use 97 percent for the interest in year 1.

   Please note: Before making an investment decision, you should check your approximate figures with a tax expert.

9

How to Survive
a Credit Crisis

Economics is cyclical. In an earlier chapter, we saw that a historical use of credit was to smooth out those cycles for farmers. Today credit can be used to smooth out personal financial cycles, but only if you exercise caution and pay complete attention.

No one is immune from these economic cycles, but if you are new to credit or have been trying a high risk venture, in good times you might have lost sight of the inevitable down cycle and made credit obligations beyond your capacity in bad times.

Worrying about unpaid bills is agonizing. Day after day, an overextended person fends off calls from creditors and night after night worries about paying bills. It's best to avoid being caught short. But there are times when facing a credit crunch is inevitable. It happens to the national economy, so why shouldn't it happen to individuals from time to time?

When institutions face credit crunches, very rarely do they

lose their credit. In the case of a city, for example, the price of borrowed money rises, but the capacity to borrow remains.

When a credit crunch happens on a personal level, an individual rather quickly loses the ability to borrow at any price.

To protect your credit if you're in trouble, you must:

1. Learn how to manage your credit during a personal credit crunch.
2. Try your best to avoid damage to your credit rating.
3. If your credit rating is damaged, work to sort it out later.
4. Stay calm. After all, it's just money.

What do you do when you've let your credit spending get away from you? Cut the cards? Put them in a safety deposit box that belongs to someone else? Call your department stores and admit to having abused your credit privileges? Call a credit counseling agency and get them to write all your creditors that you've overspent and ask them to be patient with you as you slowly pay them off?

What you should do depends upon the severity of the situation. Is your problem

1. Short-term, a temporary inability to meet your obligations?
2. A real crisis, such as loss of health or job?
3. A possible bankruptcy—when your debt so far outstrips your current and anticipated future ability to pay that you see no alternative but to turn to legal debt cancellation?
4. A case of possible fraud—did your lies catch up with you?

No matter what the case, you will survive the situation if you can keep it in perspective. During the recession in the 1970s, a research company estimated that at any given time 10 percent of the population would find themselves overextended and a substantial number would work themselves out of debt. With the liberalization of bankruptcy laws, more people have taken the option not to work themselves out of their debt, yet very few of us end up ruining our financial lives. In a moment of crisis, keep things in perspective and remember: There are far worse things in life than a temporary cash flow problem.

It is always better to watch your expenditures in the first place and not face credit problems, but if your money is tight, here are some tips to get over a rough spot.

To stretch your credit:

1. List all bills.
2. Note due dates and grace periods.
3. Pay bills only when they reach the end of the grace period—the computer does not know the difference as long as your payment is in before it triggers a "late."
4. Pay only the minimum due, but pay something on all your bills. Don't pay all of one bill and only some of another.
5. Don't charge anything on a due-in-thirty-days basis, as with American Express and Diners Club.
6. If you don't have enough to pay the minimum, then send something to each creditor. If you'll be able to pay next month, then don't explain. But if you feel this situation will persist for two or three months, send a note or call.

The note should be brief and to the point: "I'm experiencing temporary problems that should be resolved in two to three months. Here is a partial payment and I'll pay the full amount as soon as I can."

7. If creditors get nasty, remind them that it's illegal to hassle you at work if you ask them not to, to tell others who answer the phone the nature of the call, and to threaten to sue you unless they intend to. There are also limits on calls to your home. If you turn your problem over to an attorney, all calls must be through that attorney. Be assertive because collectors are trained to intimidate. (See chapter 5 for your rights under the Fair Debt Collection Practices Act.)

8. Get your credit report and monitor notations of late payments. If your problem is very short-term and you see it is not yet reflected on your current report, make a special attempt to pay minimum amounts on time.

9. Don't pay cash for anything if you can help it—conserve your cash to handle your minimum payments.

10. If you are charging to conserve your cash, watch out. Authorizations are called in by most establishments if your purchase is over the "floor limit," which varies. If you've been overextended for several months, paying your bill later than the due date, you may be turned down even if you are below your limit, or your card might be taken away. So watch the amount spent and avoid the automatic authorization terminal—the machine they run the card through and get a green or red light.

11. Better yet, spend as little as possible. Don't buy anything on credit that you don't absolutely need. Defer other things until this crisis has passed.

If you're really worried about your credit report and not afraid to take more aggressive action, you can refine the delaying process a little more by paying first those bills that do show up on your credit report.

If you've ordered your report, as you should have by now, get it out. Note which bills you owe that are listed on the report, and divide your bills according to these categories:

1. Current living, especially rent. Pay first so your home base is secure. Mortgage, phone, and utilities can be delayed some, but obviously not beyond the cutoff point.
2. Bills that affect credit rating. Pay the minimum on these if you can possibly manage, since once the thirty- or sixty-day late notations are entered on your report, it will be hard to get them removed. Also, in recent years, as credit has gotten tighter and creditors more strict, if one of your accounts checks your credit rating and sees a string of thirty- and sixty-day notices, they may cancel first and ask questions later.
3. Bills that will not affect your credit rating. Pay these last, because if you slide a month or two and then pay up, you'll probably keep this account plus all the others and preserve your credit rating.

The Credit Reporting Schedule on page 172 gives an idea of which credit most immediately affects your credit report. All will eventually appear if you don't pay, so these tactics are for short-term use only. If you have no other choice, use them cautiously rather than lose your credit rating.

Let's say you have stretched your credit for two to three months using the techniques outlined, and you have not been able to replace lost income or otherwise find a way to meet your obligations. That's a real crisis. You may lose a card or two, or even all of them.

Now your problems center primarily around how to handle

CREDITOR REPORTING SCHEDULE

Top Priority, Reported Every Month:

Diners Club
MasterCard
Visa
Sears

Medium Priority, Slower Reporting:

Large and medium department stores (check your credit
rating to see the last entry reported)
Airline charges
Liens or other legal problems (these are taken from court
records so will not appear as promptly, but once on are
very difficult to remove)
Auto loans (could face repossession)

Reported, But Not Taken Seriously:

Credit Union (since your credit union payment is deducted
from your salary, you have no choice but to pay)

Will Not Appear on Your Credit Report at All (Unless They Go
to Collection, Suit, or Judgment):

American Express
Dentist
Doctors
Electric bill
Lawyers
Mortgages
Oil cards
Rent performance (unless default)
Telephone bill

the bill collector so that you can preserve your personal sanity and your privacy in order to get back on your feet.

Even at this advanced stage, you may still be able to preserve your credit too, if you continue to follow the points outlined on pages 169–170. The name of the game here is time—remember the time value of money! You are trying to delay the creditor from taking each sequential step, because time is on your side. With luck on your side too, you may be able to defer the crisis long enough to weather it.

Although there are variations in this scenario, in a period of crisis stretching over several months (or years), you may experience the following:

- Initial collection call or letter
- More urgent calls, letters, and mailgrams
- Warnings that your credit will be canceled
- Canceled credit
- Warning that the credit will be turned over to "collections," which may or may not be an in-house agency. The collector cannot falsely claim to be an outside agency if it is in fact not one.
- Referral to collections
- Collections will repeat the same process
- Threat to refer to attorneys and sue
- Referral to attorney
- Attorney will attempt to collect again
- Service—in most states, a summons must be served, but sometimes unethical creditors fail to serve these in person
- Default judgment (if you don't appear, you will be automatically assumed to owe the money)
- Suit
- Judgment

- Collection through repossession, wage garnishment, or bank account seizure

A note of warning: This list is not exhaustive nor is it meant to be. It's just an indicator of the number of steps that occur beyond ordinary credit troubles. At each step in this process, you can simply pay (if you have the money); therefore, your goal is to delay as long as you can at each point so that you will have the maximum opportunity to get on your feet and pay your debt.

At this stage, you need to focus on generating the income necessary to meet the obligations. That means keeping yourself emotionally uninvolved in the crisis—and that certainly isn't easy! Communicating continuously with your creditors to let them know you're still actively concerned will be your hardest task. As you do so, keep in mind that collectors are just ordinary low-paid working folks who go home at night and worry about their own bills. Remember, it's likely the collector you're talking with is probably paid less than you to do a nasty job and his own survival depends on getting your money paid.

Communicate in a friendly, factual way. Don't be defensive, and stay calm. Part of the collector's bag of tricks is to make you emotionally vulnerable. Being behind makes an honest person feel guilty, and that guilt can lose you your negotiating power. If you stay detached and in control, you'll be able to negotiate better and achieve your own desired result—which is to stall until you can pay or work out a payment plan.

Even though the law and many company policies are designed to protect you, discrepancies between formal policy and informal practice often result in abuses. If you can catch a collection agency employee who has stretched her or his informal tactics beyond legal or company limits, you may be able to countersue. Although suing is expensive, sometimes just the threat of doing so will stop a creditor who is in the wrong. It pays to take careful notes to protect yourself, as the following case illustrates.

The head of a California credit counseling service told this story:

> "We received a call from a 'Blue Card' cardholder who had the card for a few months and lost her job. She had become a nervous wreck and had run up $2,000 on the card. Part of it was for necessities to keep going while unemployed, but part of it was for luxury items. Unfortunately the collector threatened to prosecute for fraud. She called us talking about suicide. We had to put her in touch with the suicide hotline.
>
> "When notified of this possible violation of California extortion laws—for that's what the collector's treatment was—the company said that this behavior violated company policy."

Imagine my surprise several months later when a similar call came into our hotline. A woman was very upset, almost hysterical. She had run up a higher than usual bill at the very same "Blue Card" company and they had accused her of fraud. She was panicked at the thought of being convicted for fraud and going to jail for putting too much on her charge, and then losing her job.

I want to show you exactly what happened, partly so that you'll know what to expect if you're ever late.

After not paying her bill the first month, our client received a past-due notice. After the second month she got a collection call, which she didn't return. Ten days later, this mailgram arrived:

YOUR PAYMENT IS DUE ON THE FIRST DAY OF THE MONTH AND BECAME DELINQUENT ON THE SECOND.

YOUR PAYMENT HAS NOT BEEN RECEIVED BY THIS OF-
FICE. TO AVOID FURTHER ACTION, IT IS IMPERATIVE THAT
YOU CONTACT THIS OFFICE IMMEDIATELY.

She was contacted by phone and mailgram again, then a
letter came informing her that the account had been turned
over to an outside collection agency. The agency was persistent—and nasty. A collector from the agency eventually accused
her of fraud, which prompted her original call to me.

I recommended that she see our credit project attorney,
who, in turn, had her call the collector and take notes. The collector repeated his illegal charge of fraud. When our client
asked, "Why would I be guilty of fraud?" His answer was, "Because you ran up such a large amount of credit. No one runs up
such a large amount without paying it within thirty days. Obviously you do not have that amount. What else can we believe
than that it was done intentionally?"

Then our consumer inquired, "What are the total ramifica-
tions, how fast will you proceed against me?"

The collector: "It would vary—how fast it is acted on here,
how fast the courts are."

The attorney knew what the hapless consumer did not:
that the consumer should have been given the opportunity to
make a repayment plan that she could meet and, more importantly from a legal point of view, she could now threaten to sue
for extortion. Because her rights had been violated, now she
could negotiate from a position of strength. She was able, with
the attorney's help, to settle for a payment plan she could handle, 6 percent of the outstanding balance per month.

Not everyone is fortunate enough to get to an attorney like
the one who served our credit project, but if you find yourself
at the collection stage, think about getting help—if only to keep
up your morale.

First, try to get a friend to sit with you and dial the phone.

Your secretary (she probably already is well aware of your circumstances), your spouse, or a relative could do it.

But, do keep in touch. As long as you can stand to handle it and there is a reasonable chance you can pay soon, delaying tactics combined with frequent communication are the best course of action.

There will come a day when you need more professional help if you haven't resolved your problem. Then you have two choices, either a community agency or an attorney.

Nonprofit community organizations, such as Consumer Credit Counselors, will, for a small fee, deal with your creditors for you. Usually, because of their community clout, they can work out a plan along the 6 percent lines discussed above.

A couple of warning notes are in order. Since often their financing comes from the lending industry, community agencies may discourage bankruptcy. In some cases, this policy could be a disservice to the consumer. Also, consumers report that counseling agencies fail to make clear the impact of their plans on consumer credit records. The fact that you use such a service is reflected on your credit record, and creditors know this notation indicates that you were in trouble. Since restoring your record is difficult, don't resort to such a service unless you've tried first to cope on your own and failed. (See the telephone directory for agencies in your area.)

For those with means, it would be better to use an attorney. Debt reorganization is a formal option open under the bankruptcy laws, but many times an attorney can arrange informal reorganization. If you are a person of property or professional standing, and you are experiencing a real but temporary crisis, you should turn to an attorney. A retainer will be required unless you are a long-standing client, but your last $1,500 might be better spent on getting high-level relief with a chance of future credit than spent on settling with one or two creditors and leaving yourself with no plan to solve your overall problem.

At some point it may become obvious to you and your advisors that even professional stalling won't help. You just do not have the resources to set up a reasonable repayment plan. If that moment arrives, you may have to explore relief under the bankruptcy laws. In addition to outright bankruptcy, there are wage earner plans offered that carry less stigma and provide payment plans combined with some debt forgiveness.

If you are thinking about bankruptcy, remember that you can keep more of your assets than before 1978, but since bankruptcy has been made easier, it seems to carry a greater stigma with potential creditors, who view with disfavor those whom they see as too willing to use the law to unfair advantage.

Also, bankruptcy will not absolve you of all your debts. Some that will remain include tax liabilities, alimony, child support, and debts resulting from intentional injury to persons or damage to property, or those obtained through fraud.

On the positive side, bankruptcy could allow you to start over as far as most of your debts are concerned. And remember, by law it stays on your record only ten years now.

Obviously you'll want to avoid this course of action if you can. Women calling our hotline are never able to get credit after a bankruptcy. Even when the case involves a wife who had little say in the decision, her credit is ruined.

Try your best to see a reputable attorney specializing in bankruptcy. Avoid do-it-yourself kits, along with ads for bankruptcy attorneys. By asking your friends, family, or a tax person, you can locate an attorney who will see you at least once to discuss your situation. If you can't afford this attorney, ask her or him for a list of community service agencies or attorneys that do pro bono (for the public good) or free work.

Once you've had a chance to talk to a professional, you'll feel better. Even if the situation seems complex to you, another person can objectify it and put it in perspective. And, if an attorney is representing you, the Fair Debt Collection Practices Act says all contact must go through your attorney. So the collectors will be off your back, and with this room to breathe, you may be able to solve your problem.

Not surprisingly, the bankruptcy system ties into the tax system. If you declare bankruptcy, the creditor can write you off as a bad debt. Unfortunately, there comes a point along the way when some creditors appear to prefer that solution. For you, it's better to let the attorney threaten bankruptcy action and hope that the creditor will eventually back down to a long-term payment plan or possibly write you off as an uncollectible debt without bankruptcy.

If a person manages to get overextended through fraud, then it's another story. If you are ever tempted to lie on a credit application, don't. If you can't pay the debt so obtained, you could be prosecuted for fraud.

Sometimes the temptation to embroider the truth comes from employees of the potential creditor, especially if the "loan officer" is, in effect, a salesperson. If employees encourage you to omit details or upgrade your income, take your business elsewhere, as this outfit isn't reliable. By encouraging you to lie, they hope to make the sale and to prevent you from defaulting through bankruptcy.

Since it is sometimes so difficult for women to get credit, we may be tempted to try to stretch the truth. Some moral justification can even be made for this position along the lines of St. Augustine's dictum, "An unjust law is no law at all." One could argue that although the law is now just, men do not justly practice it.

When faced with a system that seems to be stacked against the consumer, the temptation to lie, or at least engage in "number manipulation," is great. As we have seen, accounting rules do leave some room for interpretation. By all means take full advantage of accounting practices that may help your case. Use your gross income, and show your possessions at current market value. But don't allow yourself to be carried away. If a creditor requires that a customer live in one place a year in order to obtain credit, and you have been there seven months, it's better to wait five months. Similarly, if a creditor would consider your income sufficient if it were $1,000 per month and you have $900, try to convince them to accept your lesser amount.

There are other ways in which the application system can be manipulated, not all of which belong in the category of tactics or "accounting methods." You should avoid: sins of gross omission; changing facts, such as income; arranging for others to lie, such as about income; and falsifying supporting documents, such as income tax returns. Although the holes in the credit system make it easy to lie, the costs to you will be high in the long run.

The effect on the woman who tells the lie can be devastating, especially if the particular credit application is part of a series of financial untruths. Merely keeping track of the supporting details necessary to keep such a fiction alive can be a time-consuming task. Living with financial lies can deprive a person of a sense of security, and can have profound unanticipated effects that may return to haunt the perpetrator.

Women who undertake to obtain credit by these means should be well aware of the possible consequences, both in emotional and legal terms. Many people do lie, but I do not recommend it.

If you have been unwittingly led into a situation in which you have stretched the truth, your best bet at this stage is to be sure not to default on your obligation. If you find yourself accused of fraud, see an attorney at once.

If you get into credit trouble, whatever the cause, no matter how desperate your situation, nothing is forever. You'll be able to sort it out one way or another. Even if you have no choice but bankruptcy, remember, the writers of the Constitution thought bankruptcy was sufficiently important to provide that Congress had to make bankruptcy laws. And, many famous and otherwise successful people have lived "hounded by their creditors."

Credit difficulties are the "down side" of taking risks. Since women have not been traditionally trained to take financial risk, comparatively few women have ruined their credit through risk taking.

But taking risks is often the key to making money.

Statistics show that women are entering business in increasing numbers. Women usually form these businesses based on their own personal assets, whether savings, real estate, inheritance, or as in the case of so many women, their own credit.

Whenever you take a leap into business based on your own credit, you always risk the chance that your own personal credit might be affected if your business experiences cash flow difficulties.

Like many women, I used my own credit to start my severely undercapitalized business, and learned the hard way about the pros and cons of taking risks. Each person must learn her own tolerance for these pressures. And many of us who are new to this game must learn to expand our capacity to play by rules set by men.

The notion that these rules are learned on the playing fields is borne out by a competitive athlete turned entrepreneur, Sheila Cluff, a successful California spa owner. Sheila talked about the risks involved in starting her fitness resort business, the Oaks at Ojai.

CLUFF: When I started the Oaks, I had twelve guests in our spa hotel, which could handle eighty people. That is very scary. And the house census didn't go up according to our projections. So we used more capital initially than we anticipated in order to cover our costs and keep the doors open.

About the fourth month we started to see a turn-around, but up until then it was like a bottomless pit. We were pouring $1,000, $2,000, $3,000 a day into the operation, and quickly using up our reserve, which we had estimated would be a very good cash cushion. On the other hand, would we have been as successful if we had had more of a cushion to fall back on? Would we really have been as driven as we were when we had so much at stake?

I think this is where risk taking comes in. You have everything at stake and you really don't have any choice. You move ahead, or you totally fail. There is no gray area.

CARD: Did something in your background prepare you for risk taking?

CLUFF: I think risk and failure go hand in hand, and so do risk and success. As a competitive ice skater, I learned if you're going to compete, you have to take the risk of failing. Regardless of how hard you work, how hard you practice, and how perfect your routine is—whether it's bumpy ice, a partner that's got a cold, or a judge that doesn't like you—there is a risk that you may not be successful in spite of all the hard work and the hours you put into it.

I feel that my experience as a competitive athlete helped me develop a sense of coming out from under when things were really bad.

Risk taking is looking at and knowing that potential exists because of the risk. I learned that not all audiences were going to like me, that not every competition was going to be a success for me. So I took some personal risks, risks as far as my ego was concerned. My ability to cope with defeat, as well as my ability to handle success, comes from this experience.

The points Sheila makes are critical. Many times you can tough it out. Certainly it's better to try to see your way through very difficult situations than to fold too soon.

A final thought: to quote the bestselling title, "Tough times never last . . . but tough people do!"

TEST TO SEE
IF YOU'RE OVEREXTENDED

1. Are you behind regularly in paying your bills?

2. Is your paycheck committed before it comes in?

3. Do you know what percent of your monthly income goes to interest?

4. Do you routinely have to go to more expensive places so you can charge because your cash is low?

5. Do your bills cause you to dread opening your mailbox?

6. Do collectors call you regularly?

Solution:

1. If you get a tax refund, take a higher withholding and retire debts with this extra monthly cash.

2. Find two places to cut back some. (Like dieting, don't go overboard or you'll binge and splurge.)

3. Leave your credit cards at home so you'll have to think carefully before charging.

Conclusion

Credit is a part of life. As this book has pointed out, until recently women weren't able to participate fully in credit systems in industrial societies. Today, women's credit access is becoming a major issue in the developing world as well.

Credit is important because it represents a community's belief in the financial status of the individual. A person who has credit rates; a person who does not is a financial nonentity.

If you've never been able to get credit, you might still be skeptical. Will the techniques in this book work for you?

The answer is yes. The person who gets credit is not necessarily the one who is most qualified, but the one who knows the most about how to get it and use it.

After operating the credit hotline for several years, I decided to do a follow-up study to see how people were doing. Not every story was a success story, but some women had indeed learned about how to get credit.

In their own words, women reported about great successes and small victories.

Success Story #1: A divorced woman on disability got credit, but not without a struggle. Initially, a creditor would not give her a gas credit card, but, she reported, "Then I requested new credit cards in my own name, based on joint credit established while married (we had excellent credit). When I quoted the new laws and mentioned your organization, I promptly received the cards!"

Success Story #2: "Having worked before marriage in 1939, I was aware of the problem of nonworking wives and tried unsuccessfully to establish credit in my own name. Our joint credit has always been A-1. Now several joint accounts are reported separately as requested. We also have one short-term bank account in my name only."

Success Story #3: "Immediately after my husband's death, my bank, Bank of America, changed my Visa to my name—no hassle, no problem—even though I have not yet gone back to work. We had a $1,500 bill outstanding and all I had to do was state I would be responsible for paying. I haven't changed the name yet on other credit cards. Will do this when I have a job. Keeping fingers crossed."

Success Story #4: "My TRW had been altered and my husband's too. He had my good credit, I had his bad. Oddly enough, he worked for TRW. I contacted TRW and told them what was on his and they investigated. They found the reports had been tampered with and cleared my credit. At present I have Visa, MasterCard, American Express Gold Card, Saks Fifth, and the May Company. Unfortunately TRW could not prove he or someone else had manually changed my ratings."

Success Story #5: Married, retired, working as a temporary secretary, a California woman got credit in her name.

"I now have all credit cards in my own [maiden] name. it took a lot of patience and assertion, but it was worth the battle. The credit information was helpful not only to me, but I shared it with my women's study group at Saddleback College in Mission Viejo. We photocopied sections which were especially pertinent for our discussions. I quoted from it when the department store said it was not possible to issue me a card in my own name, which was different from my husband's. The day the last card came in the mail (incidentally it was addressed to my husband), we celebrated with champagne!"

The importance of credit is reflected in its frequent use in our newspapers to indicate a positive balance in someone's favor. With all these people claiming credit, don't you want to claim some, too?

You can get the credit you deserve! But remember to keep the following information in mind:

1. The less you need credit the easier it will be to get it.
2. The less you look as if you need credit, the more likely you are to get it.
3. Most lenders would rather loan money to someone they already know.
4. You must identify and meet the person who has the power to give you a positive credit decision.
5. Getting credit takes time.

To start the process, fill in the Credit Checklist, page 193, with your thoughts about your credit situation. (Include the book page numbers for reference, so you can find your ammunition as you go out into the field!)

People with financial clout know that credit provides powerful benefits. These include: cash flow flexibility, tax shelter benefits, and the opportunity to use capital for growth and credit for expenses. Credit also provides access to leverage and it allows you to take advantage of the time value of money.

Successful people and businesses use credit every day. Women who have managed to beat the system by joining it take advantage of credit benefits much as corporations do. The examples here in this chapter should have convinced you of the fact that women can learn the rules and win by applying them.

Businesses must have credit to function. The tax system allows deductions for interest paid. Consumers too can take advantage of these provisions. What's more, they should.

Everyone, no matter how unsophisticated an investor, needs credit. Whether you wish to get involved in the system or not, you are involved. Every time you pay for something you are either using or neglecting the opportunity to build a good credit rating. The price of ignorance could be a bad credit profile or no credit profile. By knowing what you are doing, you can join the "credit rich."

As our world rushes toward the electronic future, having a financial identity will be even more of a vital necessity. Those who do not have a financial identity may be shut out of many transactions.

There are obvious areas where change is needed in the credit system, including credit reporting, credit evaluation, marital status and the law, and tax policies as they relate to credit.

A closed system does not belong in an open society, especially not when it affects people's economic lives so completely. Why not reform the reporting system to require that consumer reports be voluntarily amended by consumers, since it is by exploiting information about these consumers' private lives that the bureaus make their money?

One enlightened Boston credit bureau is on the right track. For a small fee, they will add on any information that consumers pay to have investigated, and list accounts that do not appear. Why can't industry giants like TRW do the same?

Why not go a step further and give consumers a choice in which bureau will keep their private financial information? Our privacy laws are very strict—most financial institutions cannot report your information to third parties without your permission. But when you apply for credit today, in effect you give that permission. What if, instead, consumers could elect to subscribe to credit reporting services? They could also pay to have other information entered that would not necessarily be picked up by an ordinary credit report, such as court records pertaining to alimony, child support, information about their income—accurate up-to-date correct information thoroughly checked out by the subscriber service itself.

To go even a step further, if a consumer subscribed to one service, others could be prohibited from gathering any information but the name of the service the consumer used. Then credit bureaus would be a lot more responsive to their consumer customers instead of making fortunes off us and offering busy signals and remote offices in return!

Of course, it is possible, with the coming of the debit society and all the other new financial arrangements, that the credit reporting system will be bypassed by direct electronic reporting from the consumer's home video banking terminal directly into a centralized credit reporting computer. But, this computer would not solve other problems just cited. In fact, if our finances advance to the point of being all on one computer, we ought to demand more control over the reporting process or we will exchange convenience for complete loss of privacy. As our financial lives get more complex, our need for these protections rises. It is time that a system is developed that will provide protection for the creditor as well. That's you and me!

Credit bureaus would argue that such practices will undermine the integrity of the system, since now the system relies on the assumption that most consumers will never order their credit reports. Even if they do, they probably will not make the link between what is in the report and what they have to do to protect their credit. As consumers learn how to manipulate the credit reporting system, the value of the credit report as a predicting tool drops drastically. Why not convert this tool to a cooperative rather than closed effort?

Changes are also needed in credit scoring and evaluation. Potential consumers do not know what is required to obtain credit, so a woman has no way of knowing whether her denial was based on discrimination or actual lack of financial means. There are several specific revisions that would help. Why not make credit scoring systems public and require disclosure by law? Couple this with a requirement to tell a consumer what in her own history renders her ineligible and how she can change it.

For women and minorities, credit scoring systems should have been an improvement, for they raise credit decisions out of the subjective judgment level to "neutral" statistical bases. (No more "leg loans," an old banking phrase for an occasional loan made to a pretty woman.) But the problems with statistically valid scoring systems are comparable to those of actuarially valid insurance rates. All such numerically based systems rest on judgments, and judgments are invariably subject to bias.

Unfortunately, companies that make their money from developing scoring systems do not make the systems public, the reasoning being that consumers would try to manipulate them. If one assumes that statistically significant numbers of consumers would cheat given the chance, then, as we've seen, the credit system has weaker points than do scoring systems.

The proposed solution would substitute openness for secrecy, a change that would be more in keeping with our democratic system. Traditionally, people were fairly aware of who could get credit and why. As our society has become more complex and less personal, credit granting has developed an aura of mystery.

As we've seen, a third area in which additional help is needed, especially for women, is in the impact of marital status on credit. Even though the Equal Credit Opportunity Act and Regulation B went a long way toward solving women's former problems, several additional measures are in order. First, all credit reporting bureaus in community property states (that's 20 percent of our nation) ought to be required automatically to report credit for both spouses under both their names without further prompting from the consumer. As discussed in chapter 4, if a consumer is liable, then credit should be reported. Since community property creates mutual liability, there's no excuse for mutually exclusive credit histories.

Since it's evident that consumers don't always get credit for their credit, additional information telling them how is also in order. Creditors could easily be required to print a notice on bills, right alongside the change of address form, that allows a consumer to check if "user" reporting is desired.

More education is needed, too, so that women will make sure to have credit in their own names and to recognize a violation. Often just pointing out a problem will cause a reversal.

The need for regulation and enforcement where education fails is apparent from the abuses cited here. Especially on the federal level, in recent years, budget cutbacks have been at the expense of the consumer. Make clear to your representatives that you object to cutbacks that undermine the enforcement of your rights.

The relationship between the tax system and credit is also crucially important. Since tax "deductions" are in reality tax "expenditures," we women taxpayers ought to demand that the tax laws include more deductions of direct benefit to us, like child care and renter's deductions. These ideas aren't new, but now that you've seen exactly how the deductions work, you can appreciate their importance to you.

We also ought to ask whether tax laws do not encourage creditors to be more aggressive in order to realize their tax write-offs if consumers file bankruptcy. After a certain time has passed, it's more cost-effective for the creditor to receive a tax write-off this year—a perfect illustration of the time value of money—than payment four or five years hence. For the consumer, slow payment over a long period, while difficult, will ultimately prove less painful.

Even without needed policy changes, the credit environment will be different tomorrow. With home computers, your bank will be in your living room and you'll be able to conduct most financial transactions, including shopping, from home.

The credit card of the future may not be a credit card at all, but just the opposite, a debit card. When you use it, your account is electronically reduced right at point of purchase. Other new developments may include "smart cards," which "think" as well as "talk." In the corner of these cards is a silicon chip, no larger than a dime, that serves as a computerized memory.

To make a purchase you insert your card into a retailer's electronic reader. No need for checks, no need for authorization calls, and no need for cash. The card can store all this information right in the chip.

As electronics replace checks, over $80 billion will be saved from check processing annually. An average supermarket, for example, cashes almost 3,000 checks a week at a cost of 45 cents to process each check. A key question is: Who will pay for these new systems and who will benefit?

Gone, however, will be our float. "Float" is the period of time after a check is written but before the check reaches our bank and the money is actually taken. To compensate, we will have to work out a "preauthorized float" with our bank.

Whether you like these new developments or not, they appear inevitable. The usefulness of the smart card goes well beyond banking. It could replace your work identification card, your driver's license, serve as your birth certificate, and become your medical record. The federal government is contemplating using the card for income tax payments. In short, a "smart" type card will be the only card you will need to carry with you, and you will have to carry it because of all its features. Don't worry though. If lost, under most proposed systems it could be replaced, although it's obvious that the short-term inconvenience would be burdensome.

With this electronic financial future, having a financial standing will be even more critical than it is today. As society becomes more automated and therefore more autonomous, we will find that having a preestablished identity will be necessary for almost any commercial transaction.

These changes also raise issues of privacy. If all our information is centrally and readily available, wouldn't it make sense to prohibit by law access to that information, or to control it along the lines of the model suggested for credit-reporting bureaus?

Finally, and most important in the near term, we women ought to work to ensure that the credit rights we have gained in the past ten years are not eroded.

With improved earning power and with the protection of the Equal Credit Opportunity Act, women ought to experience relative ease in obtaining credit. However, many women have discovered through hard experience that the law works best for consumers who know how to use it. All of us must resist the illusion that once gained, rights cannot be lost.

Women's income continues to lag behind men's, and as more of us live longer, the social security system is threatened. Where will we long-lived women find security? Through our own efforts to manipulate our finances, whether by earning a living and investing carefully or by gaining a say in the dispositions of our husbands' incomes.

Credit is the single most critical component in starting along the path to financial independence. Since the credit game is one most of us will play for most of our lives, we might as well know the rules and play like pros.

CREDIT CHECKLIST

I have now:	*I need to do:*
1. Credit	I need: _____
_____	_____
_____	_____
2. Bank accounts in my name	Open an account, even if small
3. Credit history	
• Ordered credit report (date):	Received (date):
_____	_____
• Checked to see if all my credit is reported	Compare with bills and with husband's report if married
	_____
• Checked for errors	Note errors _____
• Disputed items not correct	Requested creditors and credit bureau to correct (date): _____
	_____

- Consumer comment inserted

  Checked comment
  _____
  _____

4. Requested reporting of all credit in my name from (date) _____

   Check that requests honored after 90 days _____

5. Denied credit recently. *Grounds:* _____
   _____

   Check to see if legal and fight back. *Plan:* _____
   _____

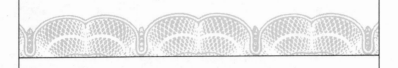

Appendixes

Appendix 1

Chapter References

Introduction

Card, Emily. "Credit for Women: The Equal Credit Opportunity Act, Operation in Community Property and Separate Property States." Typewritten. Cambridge, Mass.: Harvard University, May 1981.

Chapter 1

Report of the National Commission on Consumer Finance, Consumer Credit in the United States. Washington, D.C.: Government Printing Office, December 31, 1972.

Chapter 2

Card, Emily. "Women, Housing Access, and Mortgage Credit." *Signs, Journal of Women in Culture and Society*, vol. 5, no. 3 suppl. New York: Barnard College, Spring 1980.

Chapman, Jane Roberts. "Policy Centers: An Essential Resource." In *Women in Washington: Advocates for Public Policy*, edited by Tinker, Irene, pp. 177–90. Beverly Hills, Calif.: Sage Publications, 1983.

Gelb, Joyce and Palley, Marian. *Women and Public Policies.* Princeton: Princeton University Press, 1982.

Phillips, Diana. "Federal Financial Regulatory Agencies: Enforcement of the Equal Credit Opportunity Act." Dissertation in progress, University of Texas.

Chapter 3

U.S. Department of Housing and Urban Development, Office of Policy Development and Research. *Women and Mortgage Credit Project, Agency Enforcement and Impact Evaluation*, by Emily Card, Ph.D. Washington, D.C.: 1979.

U.S. Department of Housing and Urban Development, Office of Policy Development and Research. *Women and Mortgage Credit*: *An Annotated Bibliography*, by Emily Card, Ph.D. Washington, D.C.: 1979.

Chapter 4

Dukeminier, Jesse and Krier, James E. *Property*. Boston, Mass. and Toronto, Canada: Little, Brown and Company, 1981.

McClanahan, W. S. *Community Property Law in the United States.* Rochester, N.Y.: The Lawyers Co-operative Publishing Co., 1982, and San Francisco: Bancroft-Whitney Co., 1982.

Chapter 5

Countryman, Vern, Kaufman, Andrew L., and Wiseman, Zipporah B. *Commercial Law: Selected Statutes.* Boston, Mass. and Toronto, Canada: Little, Brown and Company, 1980.

Prochnow, Herbert V. *Bank Credit.* New York: Harper Row, 1981.

Chapter 6

Anthony, Robert N. and Reece, James S. *Accounting: Text and Cases.* Homewood, Illinois: Richard D. Irwin, Inc., and Georgetown, Ontario: Irwin-Dorsey Limited, 1979.

Chapter 8

Financial Comprehensive Mortgage Payment Tables, Publication No. 592 revised. Boston, Mass.: Financial Publishing Company, 1980, 1981.

Financial Constant Percent Amortization Tables, Publication No. 287. Boston, Mass.: Financial Publishing Company, 1975.

Appendix 2

How To Get Help

If you suspect that you have been the victim of some credit law violation, you should first contact your state attorney general's office. Most states have a toll-free number you can get by calling 800-555-1212.

Many federal agencies are responsible for monitoring the different congressional credit acts. If a question arises, listed below are the major agencies.

National Banks (Banks with N.A. or National):

Comptroller of the Currency
Department of the Treasury
Washington, D.C. 20219

Federal Credit Unions:

National Credit Union Administration
1776 G Street, N.W.
Washington, D.C. 20456

Savings and Loan Institutions:

Federal Home Loan Bank Board
Washington, D.C. 20552

State Chartered Banks that are members of the Federal Reserve System. Also, "the Fed" has overall responsibility for Regulation B:

Board of Governors of the Federal Reserve System
Washington, D.C. 20551

State Chartered Banks that are not members of the FRS, but are insured by the Federal Deposit Insurance Corporation:

Federal Deposit Insurance Corporation
550 17th Street, N.W.
Washington, D.C. 20429

Retail stores, department stores, consumer finance companies, and other creditors:

Division of Consumer Credit
Federal Trade Commission
Washington, D.C. 20580

You can also write to me at the Women's Credit and Finance Project and tell me of your experience (see Appendix 3 for address).

Appendix 3

Consumer Credit and Finance Project, and Women's Credit and Finance Project

The purpose of the Consumer Credit and Finance Project and its subsidiary, the Women's Credit and Finance Project, is to engage in research on consumer finance and to provide consumer education based on those findings.

To date the project has processed over 25,000 phone and letter inquiries.

The project was invited to prepare a Presidential Task Force Report on Equal Credit, which was presented in 1977. In 1978–79 the project produced two research studies for the federal government. In 1980, under contract to the Housing and Urban Development (HUD) Women and Mortgage Credit Project, the Women's Credit Rights Project conducted fifty seminars in Southern California. In 1979 a hotline was opened at the University of Southern California Program for the Study of Women and Men in Society and one year later at Harvard University at the Kennedy School of Government.

Write to us with problems, observations, research information about debit cards, or with your progress report (see Appendix 4).

If you need a reply, be sure to send a self-addressed envelope and $2.00 to cover administrative overhead.

Women's Credit and Finance Project
P.O. Box 10789
Marina del Rey, CA 90295

Appendix 4

Women's Credit Rights Project Follow-up Survey

Please take the time to answer the questions below and return the survey to us.

I want to remind you that under the law, court proceedings against a creditor must be started within two years from the date of the credit denial. If you believe that you were wrongfully denied credit, it is important that you get legal advice as early as possible if you intend to pursue the matter.

Please circle the number of each point that applies.

Nature of Problem or Concern　　　　*Additional Comments*

1. Need information about how to get credit.

   _____

2. Problem: Denied credit. _____
   a. No reason given by creditor. _____

   _____
   b. Insufficient credit history. _____

c. Insufficient income. _____

d. Unable to verify credit references. _____

e. Length of employment. _____

f. Excessive obligation. _____

g. Unable to verify income. _____

h. Too short a period of residence. _____

i. Delinquent credit obligations. _____

j. Other, specify: _____

_____

3. Husband's past credit problems. _____

4. Married, requested cards or credit report in my name. Creditor would not give to me. _____

5. Married, and not working now, but sought credit in my name and creditor would not grant. _____

6. Married, working, sought credit, but husband's signature required. _____

7. Married, but not working. Tried to get joint account, but creditor would not allow. _____

8. Have alimony, creditor would not count it. _____

9. Have social security, disability, or public assistance. Creditor would not count it. _____

10. Past credit problems that were serious (bankruptcy, many late payments). Need help in reestablishing credit. _____

_____

11. Other problem, please specify: _____

_____

_____

_____

12. My solution has been as follows:
    a. Do nothing. _____
    b. Go to another creditor. _____
    c. Recontact the creditor, request additional consideration. Results: _____
    d. Seek legal advice. My attorney is _____
    e. I would like a referral for legal assistance. _____
    _____

13. General comments or suggestions. Anything that you would like to share with us will be appreciated. _____
    _____
    _____
    _____
    _____
    _____

For colleagues who are doing research, please let us know about materials that you think would help us. Also, if you can send such materials, it will help us tremendously. If you are from a developing country and have special information about women and credit there, I would like to hear your news.

14. YOUR REPLY IS CONFIDENTIAL. YOUR NAME WILL NOT BE USED. Under these conditions, it will help us if you will fill out the section below so that we may keep track of your and our progress.

Name: _____ Phone: _____
Address: _____
City: _____ State: _____ Zip: _____
Marital Status: _____ Work Status: _____

15. If you would like to continue on our mailing list for further information, please check here. _____

16. If you have an attorney working on a credit matter for you, we would like to know the final outcome of your case. By signing here, you give permission for us to write the attorney and request copies of publicly filed documents.

_____   _____
Signature   Date

Please return this form to:

Women's Credit Rights Project
P.O. Box 10789
Marina del Rey, CA 90295

Appendix 5

Credit Laws Reference List

Advertising:

Credit and Leasing Costs
> *United States Code—15 USC 1661*
> *Regulation—Z*
> *Code of Federal Regulations—12 CFR 226*

FDIC Insurance
> *United States Code—12 USC 1828*
> *Code of Federal Regulations—12 CFR 328*

Interest on Deposits
> *United States Code—12 USC 1819 and 1828*
> *Code of Federal Regulations—12 CFR 229*

Consumer Credit Protection Act:

Consumer Leasing Act of 1976
> *Public Law—94–240*
> *United States Code—15 USC 1667*
> *Regulation—Z*
> *Code of Federal Regulations—12 CFR 226*

Equal Credit Opportunity Act
> *Public Law—93–495*
> *United States Code—15 USC 1691*
> *Regulation—B*
> *Code of Federal Regulations—12 CFR 202*

Fair Credit Billing Act
> *Public Law—93–495*
> *United States Code—15 USC 1666*
> *Regulation—Z*
> *Code of Federal Regulations—12 CFR 226*

Fair Credit Reporting Act
> *Public Law—91–508*
> *United States Code—15 USC 1681*

Fair Debt Collection Practices Act
> *Public Law—95–109*
> *United States Code—15 USC 1692*

Truth in Lending Act
> *Public Law—90–321*
> *United States Code—15 USC 1601*

Regulation—Z
Code of Federal Regulations—12 CFR 226

Fair Housing Act
Public Law—90–284
United States Code—42 USC 3605

Home Mortgage Disclosure Act
Public Law—94–200
United States Code—12 USC 2801
Regulation—C
Code of Federal Regulations—12 CFR 203

Interest on Deposits
Public Law—797
United States Code—12 USC 1819 and 1828
Code of Federal Regulations—12 CFR 229

Real Estate Settlement Procedures Act
Public Law—93–533
United States Code—12 USC 2601
Regulation—X
Code of Federal Regulations—24 CFR 3500

Index